ABSOLUTE BEGINNERS

Drums

BOOK TWO

WISE PUBLICATIONS
part of The Music Sales Group

London/New York/Paris/Sydney/Copenhagen/Berlin/Madrid/Tokyo

Published by
Wise Publications
8/9 Frith Street, London W1D 3JB, UK.

Exclusive Distributors:
Music Sales Limited
Distribution Centre, Newmarket Road, Bury St Edmunds,
Suffolk IP33 3YB, UK.
Music Sales Corporation
257 Park Avenue South, New York, NY10010, USA.
Music Sales Pty Limited
120 Rothschild Avenue, Rosebery, NSW 2018, Australia.

Order No. AM963633
ISBN 0-7119-8122-1
This book © Copyright 2005 Wise Publications,
a division of Music Sales Limited.

Written by Dave Zubraski
Project editor: Heather Ramage
Cover and text photographs by George Taylor
The following photographs were used with kind permission:
Ginger Baker – Ian Dickson/Redferns
Steve Gorman – Cookie Rosenberg/Retna
All other pictures courtesy London Features International
Book design by Chloë Alexander
Layout by Paul Griffin
Model: Nick Edney

Printed in the United Kingdom by
Printwise (Haverhill) Limited, Haverhill, Suffolk, UK.

Your Guarantee of Quality:
As publishers, we strive to produce every book to the highest
commercial standards.
This book has been carefully designed to minimise awkward
page turns and to make playing from it a real pleasure.
Particular care has been given to specifying acid-free,
neutral-sized paper made from pulps which have not been
elemental chlorine bleached. This pulp is from farmed sustainable
forests and was produced with special regard for the environment.
Throughout, the printing and binding have been planned to
ensure a sturdy, attractive publication which should give
years of enjoyment.
If your copy fails to meet our high standards, please inform us
and we will gladly replace it.

www.musicsales.com

Contents

Introduction

Welcome to **Absolute Beginners Drums Book Two**.

Having practised everything in *Absolute Beginners Drums Book One*, you are now ready to continue your journey and expand your drumming capabilities. As you become more proficient and your co-ordination improves, you will find it easier to learn and execute exciting new rhythms and fills.

In this book, we will cover topics including basic syncopated rhythms, two-bar drum patterns, open hi-hat beats, sixteenth note bass drum patterns, sixteenth and quarter note hi-hat patterns, drum fills around the kit, and some of the important drum rudiments.

By listening to the specially recorded audio CD, you will be able to hear exactly how the drum part should sound. Some examples are played twice on the CD – once with the drums and once without.

These tracks have been recorded by a full, live band which gives you valuable experience of what it feels like to play with other musicians.

All the examples in this book have been written assuming you are right-handed. However, if you are left-handed, play all examples with reverse hands and feet.

Before playing any of the examples in this book for the first time, say aloud the count written above each rhythm and fill. This will help you get a feel for the piece of music you are about to play, and help you get every beat exactly in the right place.

Start by playing every example very slowly and only when you feel comfortable with your playing should you try the same piece at a slightly faster tempo.

Take your time before moving on to the next example. Some parts will take more or less time to master. If you are having trouble getting a part right, always slow it down and try again.

To obtain the right feel and sound from your kit, you have to strike the drums and cymbals with enough power to create a confident and solid sound, whilst being relaxed at the same time.
This only comes with PRACTICE.

"...drums are a very important part of all cultures. The drum is something that all races have in common...A good band with a bad drummer is a bad band." Ginger Baker

Reading drum tab

Reading drum tab is easy – once you understand the fundamentals you will take to it in no time.

Drum music is written on five parallel lines called a stave. Each drum is written on a different line within the stave, as shown below.

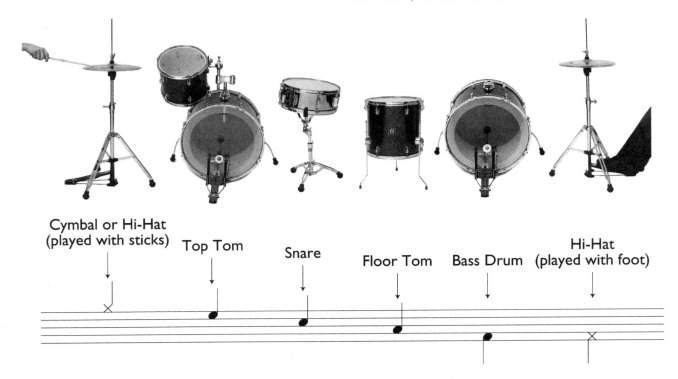

When the word "Ride" is written on the cymbal line it means the cymbal pattern is to be played on the ride cymbal. Similarly, when "H.H." is written, the cymbal pattern is to be played on the closed hi-hat (usually with your right hand).

A crash cymbal is shown with a circle around the note.

In the following example, the cymbal rhythm is played on the closed hi-hat with the first beat played on the crash.

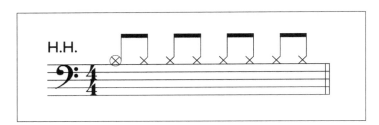

Ride cymbal

Closed hi-hat

Crash cymbal

- The main role of a drummer is to keep time. This means being able to play a piece of music from start to finish without speeding up or slowing down. It is useful to practise all the tracks in this book with and without the use of a metronome.

- Try to sit at your kit with a reasonably straight back. Slouching over your drums can lead to backache.

- Make sure you are holding your sticks correctly as shown in the picture below.

- Wear a pair of comfortable and flexible shoes or trainers.

- Set the height of the stool so your legs feel relaxed and comfortable.

- Set up your kit so everything is within easy reach.

Syncopated snare drum patterns

All the previous examples in *Absolute Beginners Drums Book One* feature the snare drum pattern falling in time with one or more of the hi-hat beats. In this section we will look at rhythms that have the snare patterns falling with, and between, the closed hi-hat beats. These are called syncopated rhythms.

In **Track 1** the sixteenth note syncopated snare beat falls between the hi-hat beats on the 'e' after count 3.

Once you've mastered the rhythm, try playing along with **Track 2**.

In **Track 3** the syncopated snare beat falls between the hi-hat beats on the 'a' before count 3.

Play along with the band in **Track 4**.

> **Tip**
>
> When playing these syncopated rhythms make sure your hi-hat plays a constant and even eighth note pattern and does not follow the snare beats.

Syncopated snare drum patterns

Here are two more variations using syncopated snare beats.

Listen to **Track 5** to hear how this should sound, then play along with **Track 6**.

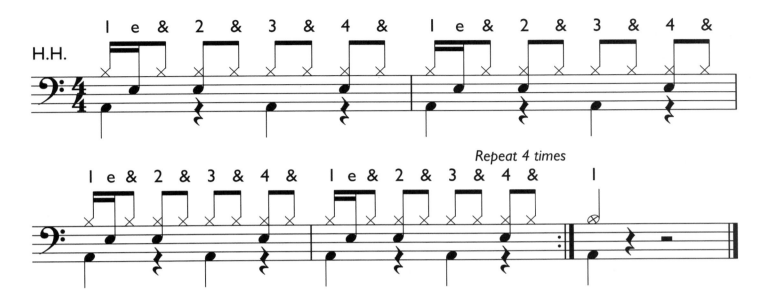

In **Track 7** there are two syncopated snare drum beats falling between the hi-hat beats on the 'a' after count '2 &' and on the 'e' after count 3.

Move on to **Track 8** to play along.

Tip

It is important to get the right balance within the kit. To obtain a good rock feel, the bass and snare drum should be equal in volume, with the cymbal pattern a little lower in volume, as you will hear on the audio CD.

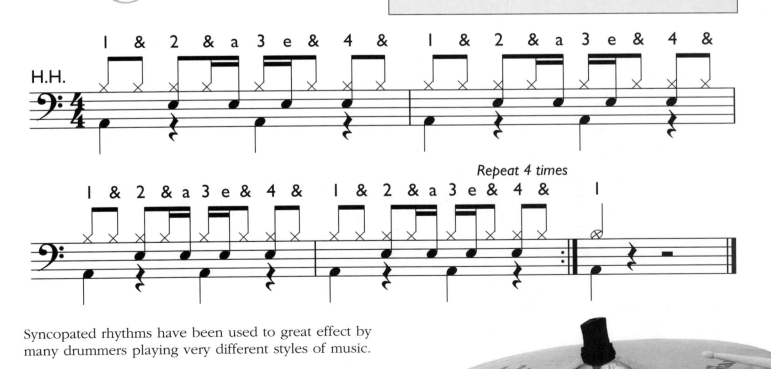

Syncopated rhythms have been used to great effect by many drummers playing very different styles of music.

They have played a big part in forming the music by artists as diverse as James Brown, Oasis, Red Hot Chili Peppers, Nirvana, and The Black Crowes.

Syncopated snare drum patterns

Syncopated snare with eighth note bass drum patterns

In the next four syncopated tracks, the bass drum gets a little busier, using quarter and eighth note patterns.

When playing these rhythms make sure your bass drum notes fall exactly in time with your hi-hat pattern.

Have a listen to **Track 9** then turn to **Track 10** and play along.

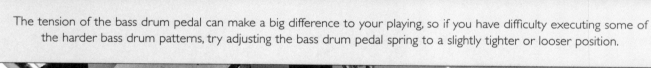

Tip

The tension of the bass drum pedal can make a big difference to your playing, so if you have difficulty executing some of the harder bass drum patterns, try adjusting the bass drum pedal spring to a slightly tighter or looser position.

In **Track 11** we have a classic example of a regularly used, exciting syncopated rhythm.

Try playing it at different tempos from slow through to medium, then fast.

Then try playing along with **Track 12**.

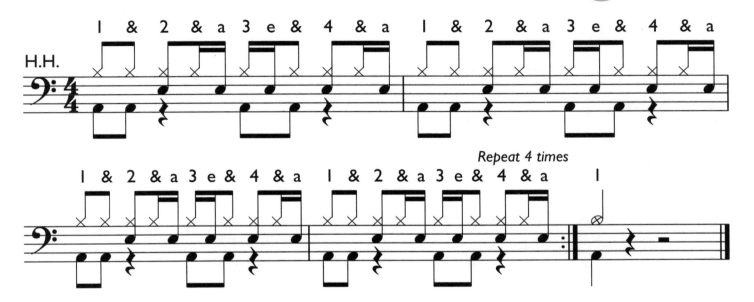

In the next two examples, we have a good example of bass guitar and drums working together.

Play **Track 13**.

Listen to how the bass drum pattern locks in with the bass guitar to form a tight rhythm section.

Once you've mastered this, play along with **Track 14**.

Syncopated snare drum patterns

Note that **Track 13** and **Track 15** have drum fills every four bars.

Track 13 has a half beat fill and **Track 15** uses a one beat fill.

Once you're familiar with the next track, play along with the band in **Track 16**.

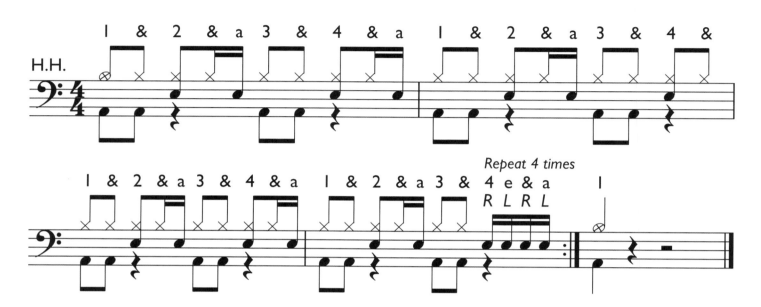

Hints & tips for successful playing

- Drink lots of water to avoid being dehydrated. It will also help your concentration.

- When it comes to practice, shorter, regular sessions are much more productive than longer, less frequent ones.

- Always stop and take a short rest before trying a new tempo. Never increase or decrease gradually (unless specified) as this will lead to bad habits later on.

- Try to sit at your kit with a reasonably straight back – no slouching!

- Keep relaxed and don't grip the sticks too tightly. This allows your drumming to flow smoothly.

- When playing in a band it is very important to listen to what the other musicians are playing, as well as to yourself. Try to lock in with the bass player by playing a similar pattern on the bass drum.

Dave Grohl's drumming with Nirvana incorporates powerful rock rhythms and fills played with a very exciting but controlled style. His use of dynamics on tracks such as 'Teen Spirit' and 'Lithium' really help to give the songs light and shade. Listen to how he chooses to play a simple, uncluttered rhythm in the verse and then a much heavier, busier, more syncopated rhythm in the chorus.

Bass and snare drum patterns

So far in all the previous rhythms, we have used only quarter or eighth note bass drum patterns. In this section we will look at rhythms using quarter, eighth and sixteenth note bass drum patterns.

In **Track 17** the sixteenth note bass drum beat falls between the hi-hat beats on the 'a' after count '2 &'. Start by practising this rhythm very slowly and be careful not to let your hi-hat pattern follow the bass drum part.

Tip

Try playing all the cymbal patterns in this book on the closed hi-hat and then try the same patterns on the ride cymbal. It is important to be able to change from the hi-hat to the ride or vice versa without losing the groove or changing the tempo.

Dotted notes: When a single dot is placed directly after a note or rest, it increases the value or duration of that note or rest by one half of its original value.

In **Track 18** the sixteenth note syncopated bass drum beat on the 'a' after count '2 &' is followed by a syncopated snare beat on the 'e' after count 3.

Tip

Try experimenting with the position of your foot on the plate of the bass drum pedal as discussed in *Absolute Beginners Drums Book One*.

Some drummers prefer playing with the foot further back on the plate when using the toes in order to get a faster action, as shown in the bottom right hand picture.

Try letting the bass drum beater rest against the drum head after each beat is played. This stops the beater from moving about between beats and helps to keep the rhythm rock solid.

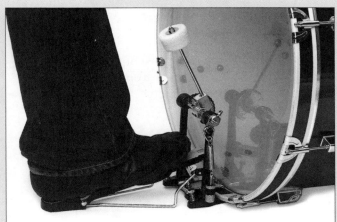

Flat Foot

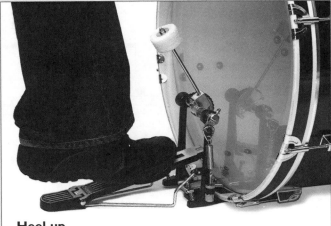

Heel up

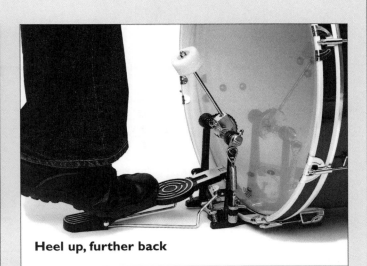

Heel up, further back

Two-bar drum patterns

So far all the previous rhythms have been played over one bar. In this section we will look at rhythms played over two bars.

In **Track 19** we have an exciting two-bar rhythm with the bass drum pattern closely following and locking in with the bass guitar.

Listen to it carefully and then move on to **Track 20** to play along.

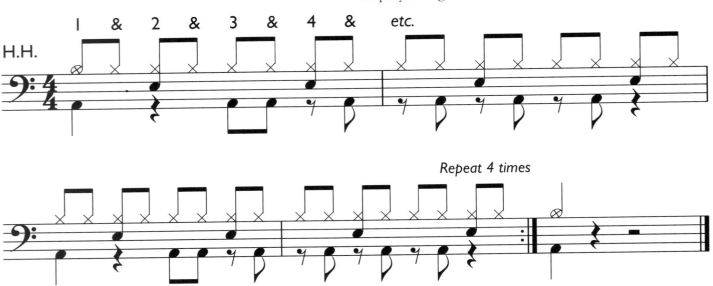

In the first bar of **Track 21** the syncopated 'a' before count 3 is played on the snare drum.
In the second bar, the syncopated 'a' is played on the bass drum.

This kind of subtle change makes the rhythm interesting while keeping the basic feel the same.

Check out **Track 22** to play along with the band.

Using two-bar syncopated drum patterns

So now, having practised all the previous syncopated rhythms we have a chance to use some of them with a full band in a longer track.

Track 23 consists of four parts (A,B,C,D).

In **PART A** we have a two-bar rhythm pattern. In the first bar, we play the syncopated rhythm as practised in **Track 21** and in the second bar we play the same rhythm but without the syncopated snare beat. Note the repeat signs at the beginning and end of this part.

In **PART B** we have another two-bar pattern. In the first bar we play a busier syncopated rhythm similar to **Track 11** but using the ride cymbal, and in the second bar we play a similar rhythm again but without the syncopated snare beats.

In **PART C** we move back onto the hi-hat and play the same two-bar rhythm as in **PART A**.

PART D is identical to **PART B**.

Practise this slowly and then once you've got it, play along with **Track 24**.

Tip

When you are playing the cymbal rhythm on the ride, you can close the hi-hat on beats 2 and 4 with your foot as shown in parts B and D.

For a good example of two-bar syncopated rhythms, listen to The Black Crowes' drummer, Steve Gorman, on 'Hard To Handle'.

Two-bar groove

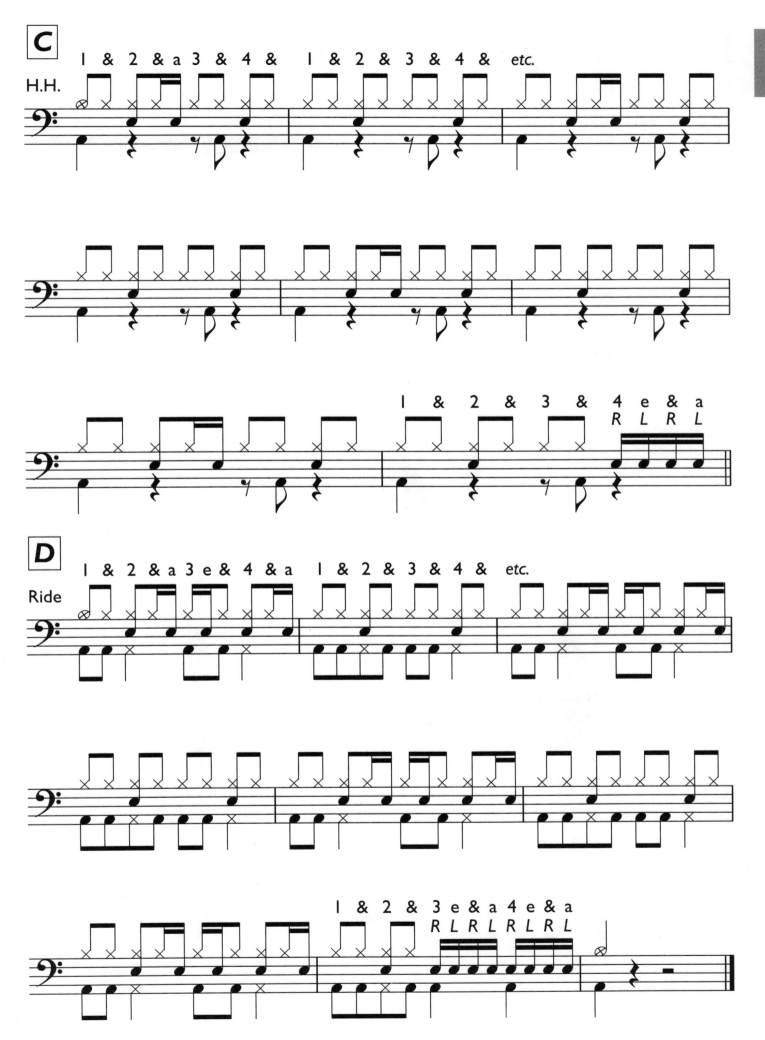

Beats using open hi-hat

When a 'o' is placed above a hi-hat note, it means that beat is played with the hi-hat cymbals open. When a '+' is placed above a hi-hat note, it means you close the hi-hat cymbals together on that beat.

In **Track 25** the hi-hat opens on the '&' after count 3 and closes on count 4 (simultaneously with the snare drum).

Tip

When playing an open hi-hat beat,
let the cymbals part only an inch or two;
do not take your foot completely off the pedal.
Keep the cymbals closed quite tightly on all other beats.
For extra practice, try opening the hi-hat on different beats
of the bar to create your own patterns.

Open Hi-hat

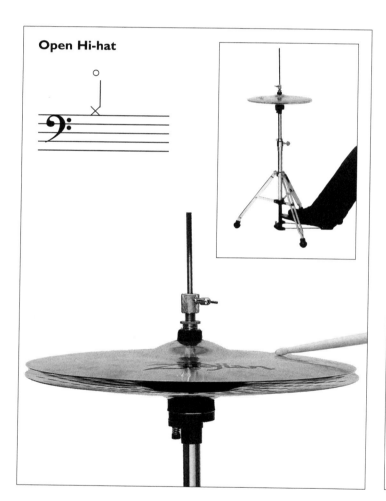

Closed Hi-hat

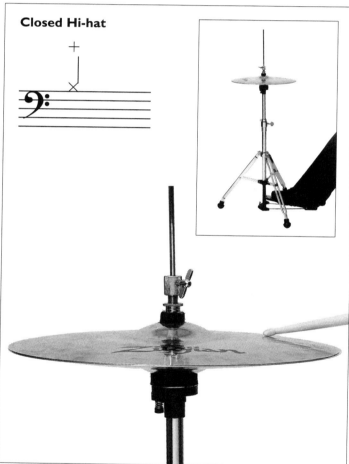

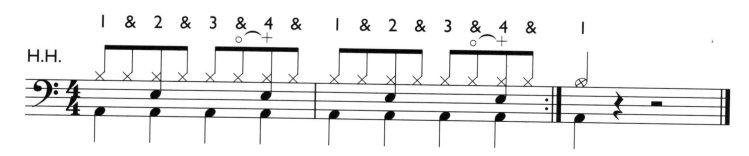

In **Track 26** the hi-hat opens on the '&' of count 2 and closes on count 3 (simultaneously with the bass drum).

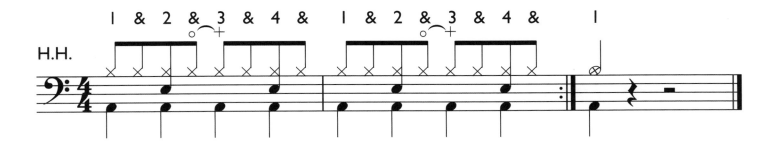

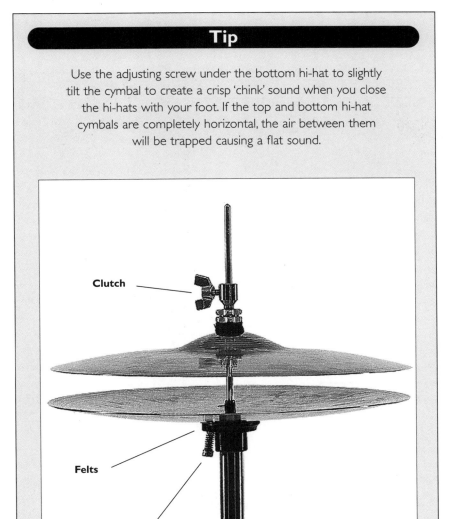

Tip

Use the adjusting screw under the bottom hi-hat to slightly tilt the cymbal to create a crisp 'chink' sound when you close the hi-hats with your foot. If the top and bottom hi-hat cymbals are completely horizontal, the air between them will be trapped causing a flat sound.

Clutch

Felts

Tilter

22

Beats using open hi-hat

In **Track 27** we have a funky syncopated rhythm where the hi-hat opens on the '&' of count 3 (simultaneously with the bass drum) and closes on count 4 (simultaneously with the snare drum).

Practise this slowly and once you've mastered it, move on to **Track 28** to play along.

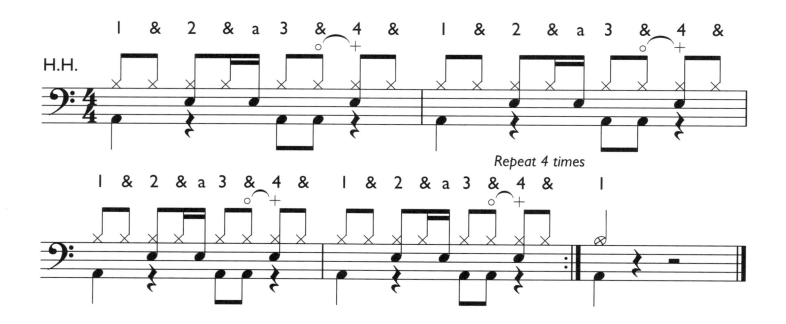

In the next example we have a syncopated rhythm where the hi-hat opens on the last beat of the bar on the '&' after count 4, and closes on the first beat of the next bar on count 1 (simultaneously with the bass drum).

Listen carefully to **Track 29**, practise, then play along with **Track 30**.

For a good example of rhythms using open hi-hat, have a listen to Chad Smith playing on Red Hot Chili Peppers' 'Funky Monks'.

Sixteenth note hi-hat patterns

So far we have only used eighth note patterns for the cymbal rhythms. In **Track 31** we have a pattern of sixteenth notes played on the closed hi-hat using single note sticking (RLRL *etc.*).

When playing these, be careful to observe the sticking: R = right hand, L = left hand.

Keep the hi-hat closed quite tight at all times and play each hi-hat beat with the tip of the stick to produce a clean, tight sound.

On counts 2 and 4, the right hand drops down to play the snare while the left hand remains on the hi-hat. The bass drum falls on counts 1 and 3.

Tip

There is a big selection of hi-hat cymbals to choose from in today's drum stores.
Many drummers prefer a pair with a heavy bottom cymbal and a lighter top such as the Zildjian 'New Beat' range.

Sixteenth note hi-hat patterns

In **Track 32** we have the same hi-hat rhythm with a different bass drum pattern.

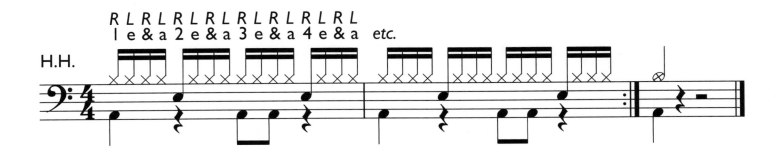

For slow tempos

When playing songs that are in a very slow tempo, eighth note cymbal patterns might feel uncomfortably slow to play, so a sixteenth note cymbal pattern is often used.

In **Track 33** below, the hi-hat pattern is played with your right hand only. The snare is played with your left hand.

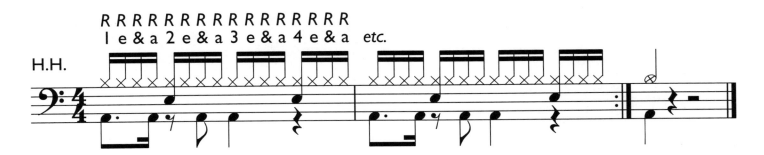

After you become comfortable playing these rhythms, try using hand to hand sticking (RLRL *etc.*) to play the closed hi-hat pattern. Make sure every bass drum beat is played exactly in time with the sixteenth note hi-hat rhythm.

In example **Track 34** over the page, we have a piece of music which demonstrates the use of sixteenth note hi-hat patterns.

In **PART A** we have a basic sixteenth note hi-hat rhythm as practised in **Track 31**.

In **PART B** the sixteenth note hi-hat pattern remains the same but the bass drum pattern gets a little busier. Note the bass drum beat falling on the 'a' after count '1 e &' coincides with the left hand hi-hat beat.

In **PART C** we play the same rhythm as in **PART A**.

In **PART D** we have a driving eighth note bass drum pattern. Make sure every bass drum beat is played exactly in time with the hi-hat beats.

When practising this track start by playing the basic rhythm (as played in **PART A**) all the way through the track.

When you feel comfortable with that, try including the change at **PART B** and finally playing the change at **PART D**.

Then go to **Track 35** to play along with the band.

Sweet sixteenth

Quarter note hi-hat patterns

In this next section we are going to use a quarter note hi-hat pattern. This gives a much heavier feel to the rhythms. As with the previous rhythms, keep the hi-hat pattern as even in sound and tempo as possible.

In **Track 36** we have the hi-hat playing a heavy quarter note pattern falling on counts 1, 2, 3, 4. The snare plays the off* beats 2 and 4 with the bass drum falling on beats 1 and 3.

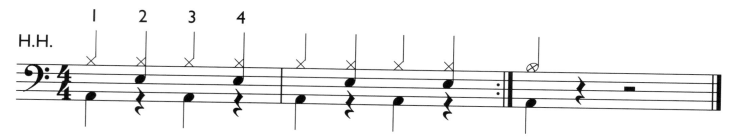

Track 37 has a more syncopated bass rhythm.

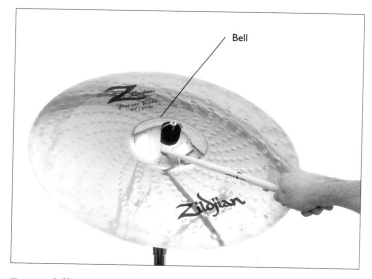

For a different sound try playing the quarter note cymbal pattern on the bell of the ride cymbal or a cow bell.

Tip

Try varying the pressure you are using with your foot on the hi-hat pedal to produce different sounds.
Having the hi-hats closed quite tightly produces a tight, clean sound but by letting the pressure off a little it allows the hi-hats to vibrate more, which gives a heavier rock sound to the rhythms.

*Beats 2 and 4 are called the 'off' beats.
Beats 1 and 3 are called the 'on' beats.

So far all the drum fills have been played on the snare drum. In this section, we will play around the kit, starting on different beats of the bar, incorporating the toms into the fills.

In **Track 38**, bar two, we have a whole bar drum fill starting on count 1. The fill moves between the snare and top-tom, then down to the floor tom.

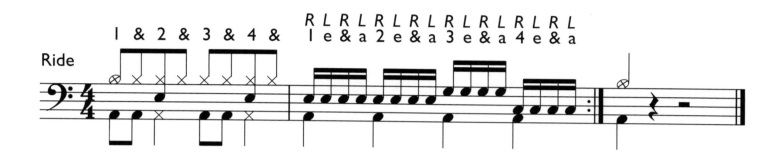

In **Track 39**, bar two, the drum fill is over two beats and starts on count 3.

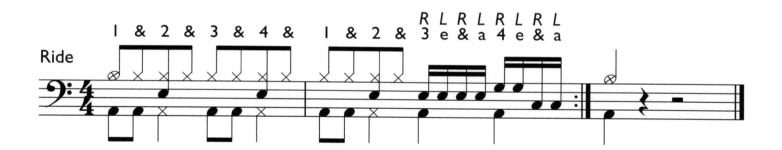

Drum fills are generally used when moving from one section of a song to another, e.g. verse to chorus, chorus to instrumental section *etc*. You will often find songs are built around sections of 4, 8, 16 or 32 bars. When you play a fill it is important to keep the tempo and groove rock steady.

Often a simple but effective one or two beat fill will flow better than a whole bar fill.

In **Track 40** we have a basic rock rhythm played for four bars using the closed hi-hat for the cymbal rhythm. After the one beat fill starting on count 4, bar four, we move the cymbal rhythm from the closed

hi-hat onto the ride cymbal for four bars. The fill in bar eight takes us back to the closed hi-hat cymbal rhythm again for the last four bars.

Listen carefully then play along with **Track 41**.

Tip
When playing fills around the kit, let your right and left sticks bounce off the drum heads to the same height to produce strong, clear, even beats.

Whole beat break

In **Track 42** we have a half beat fill starting on the '&' after count 4 every four bars.

This takes us from the hi-hat to the ride cymbal and finally back to the hi-hat for the last four bars. Move on to **Track 43** to play along.

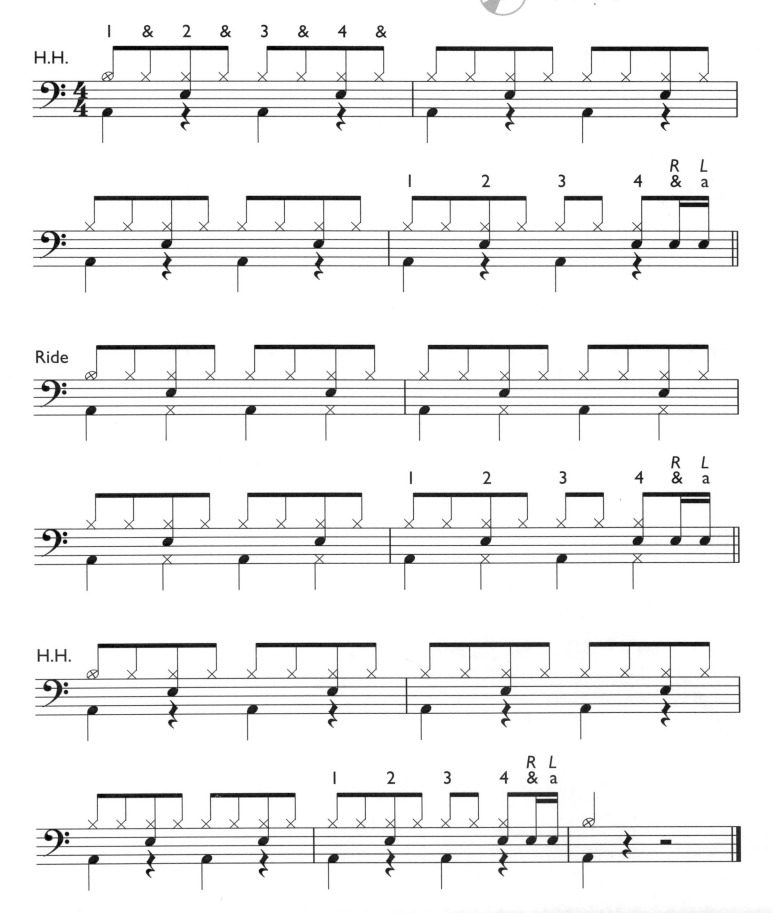

More drum fills

Drum fills using eighth and sixteenth notes

Before playing these fills, try saying the count aloud whilst playing only the bass drum pattern.
This will help give you the timing of the fill.

Have a listen to **Track 44** and then **Track 45** below.

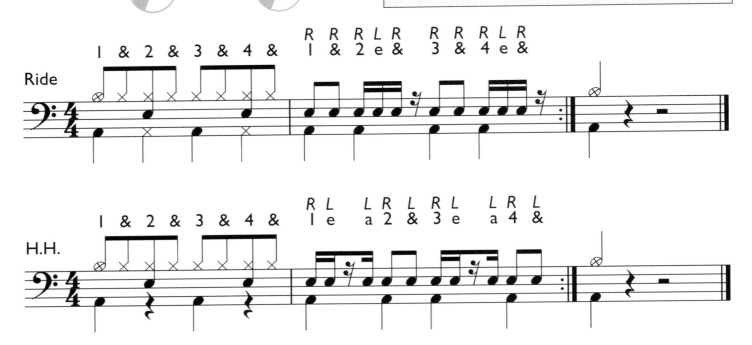

When playing these fills, keep a steady quarter note pattern on the bass drum (playing on beats 1,2,3,4). This will help keep your fills in time and add some depth of sound.

Check out **Track 46** and **Track 47** below.

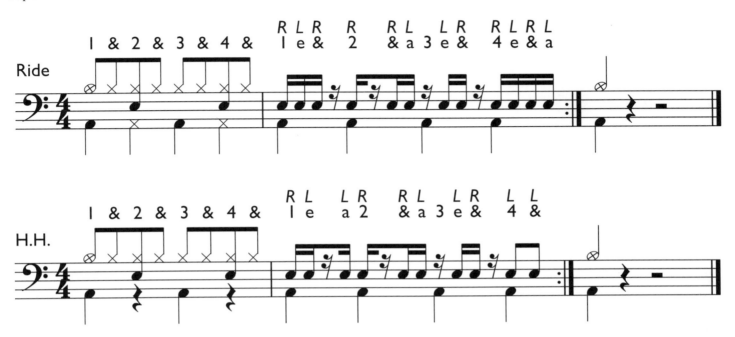

Simon Phillips is known for his stunning technique, versatility and impeccable timing. Having learnt to read drum parts at an early age, he soon began doing sessions which gave him valuble experience in playing all styles of music.

Simon has played and recorded with musicians as diverese as Jeff Beck, Pete Townsend, Joe Satriani, Toto and Stanley Clarke.

Drum rudiments

There are 13 essential drum rudiments.
In this book we will cover three of the most
important ones.

> ### Tip
>
> For extra practice, start both of the
> tracks below with your left hand, e.g. LRLL RLRR.
> Practise these paradiddles at different tempos from slow,
> to medium, to fast.

The paradiddle

This rudiment is called a paradiddle because of the
sticking used to play it: RLRRLRLL *etc*.

In **Track 48** bar A contains eighth notes and bar B
contains sixteenth notes. Make sure every beat is even
in tempo and volume.

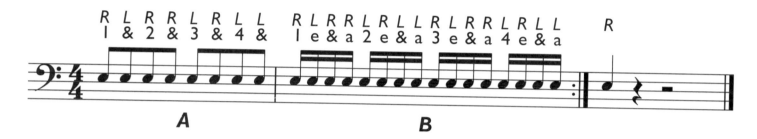

In **Track 49** we have added the bass drum (playing
quarter notes) and hi-hat (falling on counts 2 and 4)
to the paradiddle pattern played on the snare.

Track 50 has a bar of rhythm followed by a one-bar, sixteenth note drum fill played with paradiddle sticking.
Note the toms play on beats 1, 2, 3 & 4.

In **Track 51**, bar 2, we have a paradiddle played between the right foot (on the bass drum) and the left hand (on the snare).

Make sure the closed hi-hat plays a constant eighth note pattern and does not follow the bass drum pattern.

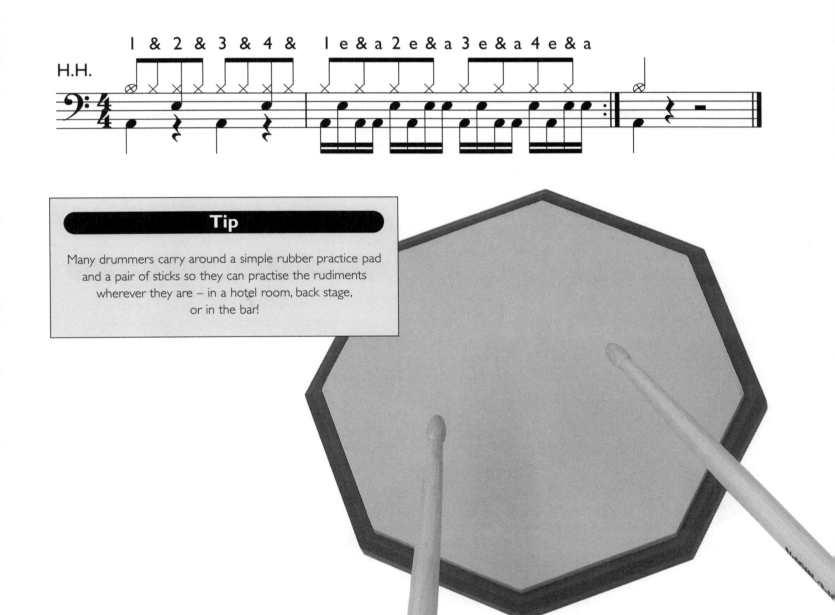

Tip

Many drummers carry around a simple rubber practice pad and a pair of sticks so they can practise the rudiments wherever they are – in a hotel room, back stage, or in the bar!

Drum rudiments

The flam

The 'flam' consists of a main (accented) note preceded by a grace note (shown as a smaller note) The grace note should be played very lightly and as close to the main note as possible. To start with however, keep the two notes apart, gradually bringing them closer as you become more proficient.

As you play the flam, start with the hand which is playing the heavier, accented note, higher above the drum head than your hand which is playing the lighter, grace note.
Have a listen to **Track 52**.

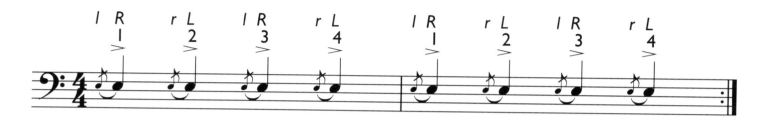

In **Track 53** we have a drum fill played between the snare and bass drum incorporating the flam.

For a good example of the flam listen to Dave Grohl playing the drum intro to Nirvana's 'Smells Like Teen Spirit'.

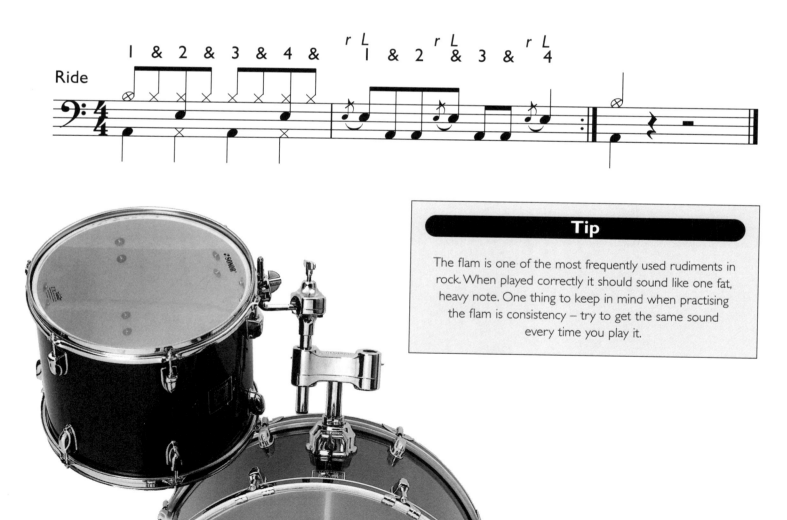

Tip

The flam is one of the most frequently used rudiments in rock. When played correctly it should sound like one fat, heavy note. One thing to keep in mind when practising the flam is consistency – try to get the same sound every time you play it.

The long double stroke roll

In **Track 54** there are no bar lines or time signature. This is because you start the double stroke roll very slowly (open) playing two beats with each hand, e.g. RRLL *etc.* gradually increasing the speed (close) then gradually and evenly decreasing the speed, bringing you back to your starting tempo.

When practising the double stroke roll, let each beat bounce back off the drum head up to the same height and make sure every beat is played with an equal amount of volume (especially the second of every double). As soon as you feel yourself becoming tense or uneven start to gradually slow the roll down.

R R L L R R L L R R L L R R L L *etc.*

Tip

Rudiments take a lot of practice to execute well. However, in order to progress and become more proficient, it is worthwhile starting every practice session going through your rudiments before anything else.

Track 55 is a piece of music constructed of four parts (A,B,C,D) featuring an exciting syncopated rock rhythm which will give you the chance to put some of the rhythms and fills we have covered in *Absolute Beginners Drums Book One* and *Book Two* into practice.

PART A starts with a basic rock beat for eight bars with the snare falling on the off beats, 2 and 4. The bass drum falls on counts 1 and '3 &' together with the closed hi-hat rhythm. The drum fill in bar eight leads us into the next part.

PART B features a syncopated snare drum rhythm similar to the rhythm used in **Track 11**, but here we play the cymbal pattern on the ride cymbal and close the hi-hats on counts 2 and 4 at the same time as the snare drum. The drum fill at the end of bar eight in **PART B** leads us into **PART C**.

PART C has the same rhythm as in **PART A** except for the fill in bar eight, which starts on the '&' after count 3. This fill leads us into the next part.

PART D has the same syncopated rhythm as in **PART A** except for the fill in bar eight, which starts with your left hand on the 'a' after count '2 &'.

Well done! Now turn over the page and listen to **Track 55**, then have a go at playing along with **Track 56**.

Drum time

Summary

Having practised and mastered all the tracks in *Absolute Beginners Drums Book One* and *Book Two*, you will have gained a valuable understanding of playing basic rock drums.

As with any art form, it is important to strive to be original, so now you can play all the rhythms and fills as written, don't stop there! Try to adapt and change them to create your own music.

Just by moving one part of a rhythm to another drum or cymbal (e.g. the hi-hat part to the floor tom) you can completely change the sound and mood of the music.

So keep your ears open, listen to other players, keep practising and above all, enjoy yourself!

Indian Classical Dance

Leela Venkataraman
Avinash Pasricha

INDIAN CLASSICAL DANCE
Tradition in Transition

Lustre Press
Roli Books

ISBN : 81-7436-216-9

© Roli Books Pvt. Ltd. 2002
Lustre Press Pvt. Ltd.

M-75, Greater Kailash-II Market,
New Delhi-110 048, INDIA
Phones: (011) 6442271, 6462782, 6460886.
Fax: (011) 6467185.
E-mail: roli@vsnl.com

Author: Leela Venkataraman
Photographs: Copyright © Avinash Pasricha

Design: Yogesh Suraksha Design Studio
         www.ysdesignstudio.com

Printed and bound in Singapore

Contents

Preface

Traditional art forms are subject to cycles of growth, decay, and renewal. After centuries of being nurtured in the temple and the court, Indian dances suffered a reversal during colonial rule. They revived during the Nationalist movement to start a dance renaissance in post-Independence India.

The classical arts have always been challenged by the dialectics of tradition versus modernity. Now the argument is prefaced by the mistaken notion that what cannot shake off the shackles of the past, cannot adapt itself to the changed present.

At no point do our ancient texts, specifically the *Natya Sastra*, the Indian Bible of dance, give cultural memory a place which ignores the compulsions of the present. The very fact of continuity recognises traditions as flowing streams from the past to the present to the future. Our ancient integrated worldview, to quote Dr Kapila Vatsyayan's book, *The Natya Sastra*, embodies a vision 'concurrently at the level of the physical and the metaphysical, the terrestrial and the celestial, the purely biological and the psychical, the sensuous and the spiritual'.

Pluralism is the bedrock on which our cultural ethos is built. We live in many ages and at different levels simultaneously. Just one visit to Chidambaram during the Arudra Festival or to Ajmer to participate in the Urs Festival at Salim Chisti's *dargah* puts the visitor in touch with the intangibles of this culture. Like the icon of the Dhyana Dakshinamurti (the mediating Siva), these remain an uncrushable part of the people's psyche.

The journey of the dance from temple and court to the proscenium has meant change. Dances nurtured for years in interior areas are now seen on the international stage. Change is inevitable and nobody would think of traditions as frozen in time. But what direction change takes is the main concern.

Exploring the dance for creating visual geometry, trying abstract works, fusing different styles, fashioning classical movement and rhythms to varied sound tracks are all part of the contemporary classical dance scenario. Today, dancers are pushing the classical forms to their farthest limits. Many artistes still feel that space for originality and creativity can be found within the conventional format, necessitating no compromise on the preserved integrity of classical structures.

One argument states that the fiercely individualistic dancer of the day cannot find her/his ideal expression in the conventional repertoire of lyrics fashioned for a patriarchal and feudal society. The counter argument holds this to be narrow-minded approach, unable to appreciate the poetic richness of our musical heritage.

Neither view is wrong. An aesthetic approach can make space for both the structured (*baddha*) and the unstructured (*anibaddha*). The danger to classicism comes not from differing views but from mediocrity and superficiality. Change for the sake of being different cannot carry conviction.

This book traces classical forms as they have journeyed from the past to the present. In the process, the challenges a globalised society poses to art are looked at. Curiously in the present context, classical dancers are seen to be increasing while audiences are shrinking. The classical dancer soldiers on nevertheless, waging an unequal battle against the monolithic mega entertainment machine – television.

Many famous dancers do not find mention in this book, which mainly looks at trends rather than individuals. Traditions are always in transition and the classical dances in this book are viewed more in their prescribed structures. The radical spin-offs have been kept outside the purview of the book, for these would require the kind of space this book does not accommodate.

I am deeply indebted to Gurus Sadanam Balakrishnan and Singhajit Singh and his wife Charu Sija Mathur, and to scholars Dr Leela Omcherry and Dr J. V. Meenakshi and also to dancers Leela Samson, Swapnasundari and Prerna Shrimali, who have all been sounding boards for my views. I have benefited greatly from interacting with them.

Bharatanatyam

urtured in the heartland of the Cauvery basin of peninsular India, Bharatanatyam is amongst the oldest of the contemporary classical dances of India. Overwhelming literary, architectural and epigraphical evidence testifies to its antiquity. But the dance in its present form is not more than two hundred years old, having had its beginnings in ancient Tamil culture mingling with the Sanskrit culture enveloping the whole of India. The origins of the dance can be traced to the *Tolkappiyam*, a work of Tamil grammar offering insights into the art and life of the people. The earliest of Tamil literature, grouped into schematic anthologies[1] contains references to dancers, both female (*Virali* or *Kuttiyar*) and male (*Kuttar*), to victory and celebratory dances and to travelling musicians (*Porunar*). *Madiraikanchi*, a post-Sangam work, mentions ritual dances and special performances in which the dancer, getting into

a trance became an oracle. Even the death of a king in battle saw the other kings stopping war games to dance round the felled body. A variety of musical instruments and the courtesans who played them, *Paraittaiyar*, are mentioned.

The earliest architectural evidence of dance in Tamil Nadu is found in the Jaina rock-cut caves. Jaina prince Ilango Adigal of the Chera dynasty is credited with composing the Tamil epic, *Silappadikaram* (*Silambu* means anklet, and *Adikaram* means story – here, the chapter). This story of the anklet, with the central character of a dancer, Madhavi, is a treasure trove of information on dance. The *Natya-Ganikai*, as the dancer is called, is mentioned as having mastered dance and the allied discipline of music for seven years before her debut or *Arangetram*[2] on a stage of prescribed measurements. The stage is a simpler version of the stage mentioned in the *Natya Sastra*,

the oldest treatise on Indian theatre, of which dance was a part. Even hand gestures are mentioned, not to speak of categories like secular dance as differentiated from ritual dance, abstract dance as separate from interpretative dance and of graceful movements as differentiated from their more vigorous counterparts – all of which points to an actively evolving art. The terminology was, of course, different, *Santi Koottu*[3] being the equivalent of classical dance, while popular forms of entertainment like gymnastics, puppetry, and clowning were clubbed under *Vinoda Kuttu*. Dance was always referred to as *Aattam* or *Koottu* and in later years, Nataraja, the King of Dance, came to be known as *Aadavallaan* or *Kuttan* – a direct derivation from these terms.

Cheran Senguttuvan of the Sangam age is said to have travelled on his long expeditions with over a hundred dancers and jesters with about two hundred musicians in tow, proof of royal support to a popular art form.

It is interesting to note that Aham poetry (expressive of love in the first person) and *Atruppadai*[4] (where the deity is glorified as a munificent prince) using a King/God concept provided the earliest model for the later *Varnam*, which even now forms the centrepiece of a Bharatanatyam recital. Here, the dancer addresses the deity as a devotee and also as a beloved, combining the divine-secular and *bhakti-sringar* approach.

Poetry as the starting point of an idea, expressed through word and metre, found its musicality set to melody. It became a visual expression in the dancer's interpretation, with arrested points in movement frozen in sculptural representation. This illustrates the give and take prevailing among all art disciplines in the holistic approach.

A world-view looking upon the secular and the divine, the manifest and the unmanifest as part of one integrated entity gave religion a pre-eminent place. Animism was followed by religions like Hinduism, Buddhism and Jainism co-existing and dominating by turns. Tamil literature flourished even during what historians refer to as the dark period from the third to the sixth centuries. Jainism, long after it had ceased to be a religious force, continued to get royal patronage during the Chola period (ninth-twelfth century). The Chola kings who were devout Saivites built special

Jinalayas beside Shiva and Vishnu temples. The trend continued under the Pandyas in the thirteenth and fourteenth centuries. The temple, one has to remember, was more than just a place of worship. It was the fulcrum of manifold activities round which townships grew, with dance and music being prime activities connected with temple ritual.

Right from the days of Karaikkal Ammaiyar (fifth century A.D.), devotional poetry had been a feature of the south. The Nayanmars[5], all Saiva saints who expounded their philosophy through hymns, and their Vaishnavite counterparts, the Alwars (sixth-tenth centuries) who sang the praises of Vishnu, left behind a legacy of devotional poems that provided a literary springboard for music and dance. Reciting the *Tevaram*, the Nayanmars' hymns, formed part of temple worship. As for the *Divya Prabandham* Alwar mystic poetry which inspired the later *Bhagavata Purana* and love poetry penned by sixteenth and seventeenth century composers like Annamacharya, Tirtha Narayana and Kshetragna, it offered rich material for dance interpretation. In the temples of Srirangam and Srivilliputtur, an uncomplicated gesture/movement/ song routine called *Araiyar Sevai* evolved as part of temple ritual[6].

With the dynasties of the Pallavas, Cholas, Cheras and Pandyas rising and falling and rising again, political contours constantly changed and migrations led to regional cultural interactions. During the eighteenth century, the Marathas ruled over parts of the Tamil country. Telugu was the official language, a hangover from the Nayaka rule of the sixteenth-seventeenth centuries. A sizeable part of the repertoire for Carnatic classical music is still in Telugu. So what one understands as a linguistic territory did not correspond to the geographical/political limits of states as existing now.

Great temple builders, the Cholas, who ruled again between the ninth and the thirteenth centuries, left a wealth of material on dance carved as inscriptions and sculptures on temples. In the earlier period, while no definite reference to the *devadasi* is known, women captured in battle called *Kondi Magalir* were commissioned to serve in temples. By the eighth century, the idea of temple dancers had evolved. Temple sculpture is replete with dance representations, sculpted in the half-seated *araimandi* with out-turned knees, the core stance of Bharatanatyam. Dance poses abound in the grand temples like the Brihadeshwara temple at Tanjavur, Gangasikonda Choliswaram temple at Gangaikonda Cholapuram, the Iravateswara temple at Darasuram, the Kampahareswara (Tribhuvaneswara) temple at Tribhuvanam, the Nataraja temple at Chidambaram, the cluster of temples at Kumbakonam and Kanchipuram and the Meenakshi Sundareswara temple at Madurai. In temples like the Nataraja temple at Chidambaram, the relevant couplet from the *Natya Sastra* (theorising movement details) is engraved under the figures in the *gopuram* passageway[7]. The dancer occupied a respectable place in society, though the religion-art interaction had its own tension. One of the Shaiva saints, Sundarar, while wandering and singing the praises of Shiva, reached Tiruvarur town, where Shiva was worshipped as Tyagesa. He lost his heart to the famous temple dancer, Paravai Nachchiyar, whom he made his second wife. The other wife, Sangili Nachchiyar from Tiruvorriyur, was also a temple dancer-devotee. Stories, not always apocryphal, of kings developing intimate relationships with temple dancers are part of Tamil history. For instance, Rajendra Chola I loved one Anukkiyar Paravai Nangaiyar[8] of Tiruvarur. The title of *Manikkam* (ruby) was bestowed upon chosen temple dancers as inscriptions tell. Near the eastern entrance to the Lord Tyagesa temple at Tiruvarur, for instance, is a shrine dedicated to dancer Manikka Nacchhiyar.

On initiation, the image of a *Soolam* (trident) was branded on the temple dancer's arm. The practice continued till the last century. In the sixth regnal year of Parakesarivarman Rajendra Chola II, an inscription mentions that 120 *kalams* of paddy were to be given from the temple store to one Santi-k-kuttan Tiruvalan Vijaya Rajendra Acharyan and his descendants. They had enacted the *Raja Rajeswara Natakam*[9], during the great Vaikasi Festival of the Lord, in the temple on a regular basis. The *Natakam* was a forerunner of the *Kuravanji* dance dramas, an important Bharatanatyam heritage.

A famous inscription of Rajaraja I at Tanjavur gives details of

400 *Talippendir* (*Tali* means temple; and *pendir*, women) as the *devadasi* was called being assigned to the Rajarajeswaram or Brihadeshwara temple and being given a house each in earmarked streets. The inscription mentions the address and the descriptive title of the temple dancer[10]. The term used was *Talippen* and in later years *Devar-Adiyar* came into vogue, meaning servant of God or *devadasi*.

After the Cholas came the Pandyas, but only till 1370. During their rule, Ibn Batuta visited the Madurai Sultanate, which had already been subject to intermittent invasions, and wrote in his travelogue about the sorry state of temple dancers in this unsure political climate. The Vijayanagara kings and then the Nayak governors were also patrons as the sculptured walls and towers of temples in Vriddhachalam and Tiruvannamalai would indicate, being full of *surasundaris* and dancing deities. With the fall of the Vijayanagara empire, a confused political period ensued with vassals proclaiming independence.

Fortunately for the arts, the period of bleakness was followed by one of the most prosperous ages, with Nayaka rule being established in Tanjavur by a chieftain, Sevappa Nayaka (1530-1580). His successors, Achyutappa Nayaka (1561-1614), Raghunatha Nayaka (1584-1634) and Vijaya Raghava Nayaka (1634-1673) were great composers and authors. It was in the time of Vijaya Nayaka that the great lyricist, Kshetragna (1610-1685), composed countless *padams* in the king's court. During the rule of Achyutappa Nayaka, Bhagavatulu families fleeing from the capital city, Vijayanagara, after the Talakota battle disaster in 1565 were provided shelter and settled in what was later called the Melattur village. It had a great tradition of *Bhagavata Mela Natakam* – an all male classical dance drama tradition still performed during *Narasimha Jayanti* in the courtyard and in the *sannidhi* of the Varadaraja Perumal temple in the village. Music parties were referred to as *Sangita Melam* and, later, the *Periya* (big) *Melam*; dance was the *Chinna* (small) *Melam*.

Close on the heels of the disintegration of Nayaka power, another golden period followed. Ekoji I established Maratha rule in the south (1676), with the rulers themselves being patrons and composers of lyrics and librettos. Strangely, the same Bhonsle dynasty in Maharashtra did not produce royal

personages with such aptitude. It was in Tanjavur that the Marathas shone as writers and patrons. Shahaji II, who ascended the throne in 1684, composed a whole repertoire of works for music and dance. A devotee of Lord Tyagesa, he wrote under the same pen name and his works are a meeting point for literature, music, drama and dance. He introduced the practice of *Sankara Pallaki Seva Prabandham* during the annual *Brahmotsavam* as part of temple ritual, involving several musicians and *devadasis*. Sarfoji I (1712-1728) continued art promotion and during the time of Tulaja (1728-1736) the dancers rendered *Sallamuru padams* as salutation to the king in court. A scholar in Marathi, Telugu and Sanskrit, Tulaja wrote *Sangita Saramrita*, listing 18 movement units called *adavus*[11], some identifiable in present-day Bharatanatyam. It was during the time of Pratapa Simha (1739-1763) that the famous *devadasi* Muddu Palani wrote the bold work, *Radhika Santvanumu*. It portrays Radha as a liberated woman and an equal partner with Krishna. A century and a half later, the work was banned for its flagrantly erotic tone and though Bangalore Nagaratnamma, a twentieth-century *devadasi* fought in court and got the ban lifted, most dancers left the work untouched. Very recently, passages from it have inspired a Kuchipudi work by dancer Swapna Sundari.

The foundation for present-day Bharatanatyam was laid when Tulaja II (1763-1787) invited Mahadeva Nattuvanar, a guru from Tirunelveli, to the Tanjavur court. He came with two dancers, Vanajakshi and Muttumannar, who presented the *varnam*, 'Bhosala Tulaja Rajendra Raja' dedicated to the king. The dance was at this time called *Sadir* or *Dasi Attam*, Bharatanatyam being a later appellation. During Tulaja's time lived the epoch-making Carnatic musical trinity, Tyagaraja (1767-1847), Muttuswamy Dikshitar (1775-1834) and Shyama Sastry (1762-1827). Their compositions still form a major part of Carnatic music.

The two *Nattuvans*[12], as the dance gurus were called, Gangaimuttu and Subbaraya Oduvar, also arrived at Tanjore and were allotted a building opposite the main temple known as Nattuvan Chavadi. After Tulaja came Amarasinghe (1787-1799) who shifted his headquarters to Tiruvidaimarudur, another famous centre for dancers and for musicians like Ghanam Krishna Iyer and Gopala Krishna Bharati. Their compositions still form the musical-textual base for

Bharatanatyam. Defying the ban on court dancing imposed by the now powerful British East India Company, the court patronised *Sadir* performances. At the *Periya Koil* (Big Temple) in Tanjore, the *Sarabhendra Bhupala Kuravanji natakam* was enacted regularly.

Subbaraya Oduvar, one of the two *Nattuvans* at Tanjore, produced four great sons Ponniah, Chinnaiah, Sivanandam and Vadivelu, who became the legendary Quartet (*Naalwar*) that designed the entire format of present-day Bharatanatyam. From 1798-1832, Serfoji II[13] ensured royal support for the arts and dances like *Pinnal Kolattam*, *Poikal Kudirai* (Dummy Horse), still very popular in Tamil Nadu, became part of the dance scene. During the days of Sivaji II (1832-1855), the last of the Maratha rulers in the south, Sivanandam of the Quartet composed the *varnam* in *Todi*, 'Danike Taku Janura', performed with great flair by the great Balasaraswati.

The Kuravanji dance drama enactments introduced type characters like the male *Singi* and female *Singar* (hunter and huntress) and *Kuratthi* (Gypsy woman) who predicts a happy ending for the princess – a pattern that became part of the stylised *Natakam* format. Kummi Kamalambal was famous for her role of the *Kuratthi*. Musical forms like the *Gitam*, *Varnam*, *Kirtanam*, *Kriti*, *Padam*, and *Tillana* had become part of dance. In the temples, *devadasis* regularly performed *Navasandhi* as a ritual addressed to the nine deities guarding the temple directions.

The Quartet's concert format of *Alaripu*, *Jatiswaram*, *Sabdam*, *Varnam*, *Padam*, *Javali*, and *Tillana* is still followed, though the *Jatiswaram* and *Sabdam* have become less common. Dancer Balasaraswati likened the progression from *Alaripu* to *Tillana* to the process of entering the temple, reaching the altar and, finally, being in communion with the deity. The *Alaripu*, which marks the dancer's entrance, is a crisp introduction to the basic grammar of movement in Bharatanatyam. Rendered to a recitation of rhythmic syllables, it has kinetic symmetry: movements fan out from and converge on to the centre of the body, with the weight balanced on both feet. It is a warming up process, like the worshipper entering the temple gateway with a mind uncluttered by the mundane concerns of life. The *Jatiswaram* introduces melody and abstract rhythms get an extension, the patterns

19

Dancer Urmila
Satyanarayanan strikes
strong *nritta* poses,
conveying power without
abandoning elegance.

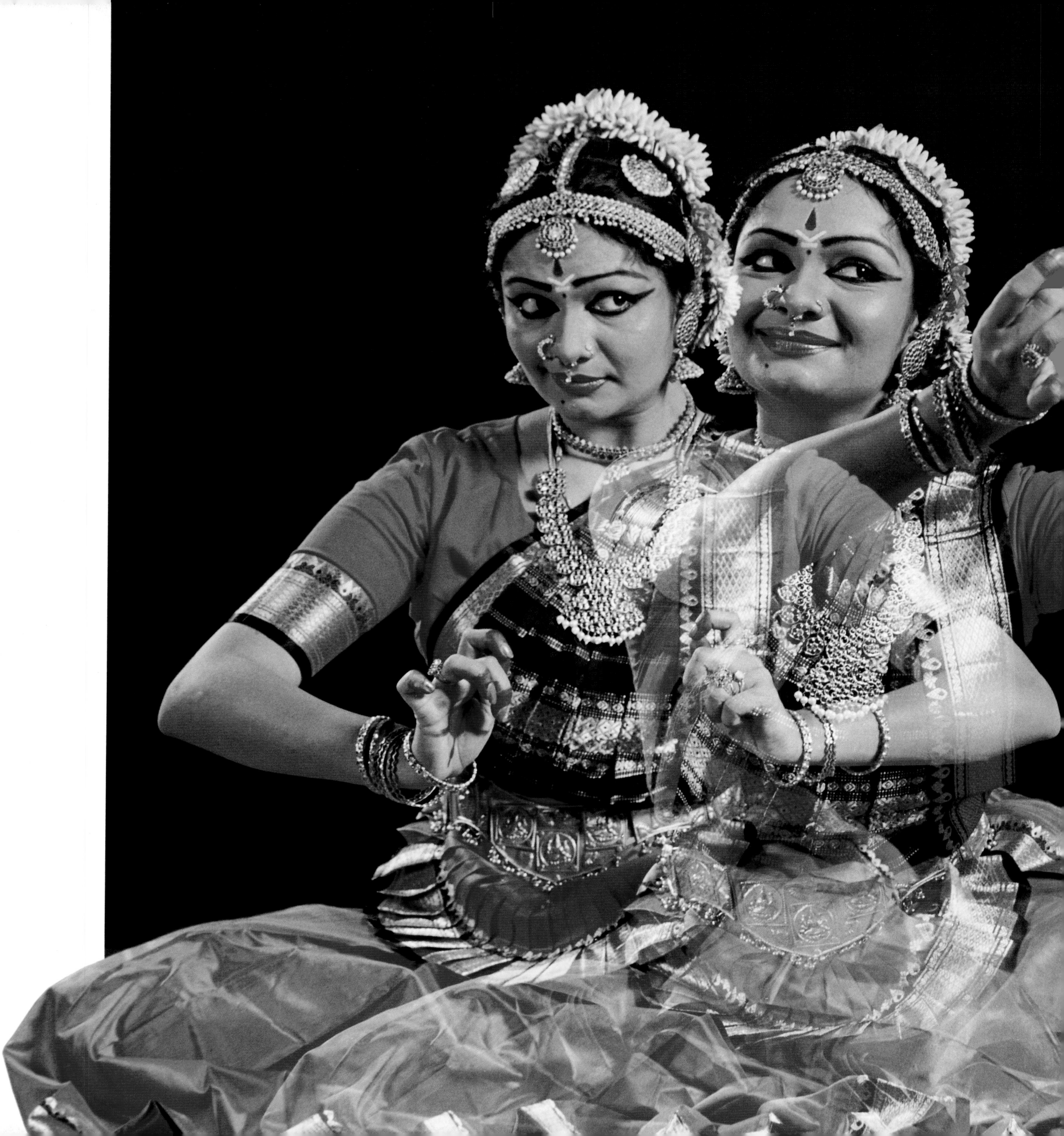

being dictated by the solfa music arrangements. This is like moving on to the *Agramandapa* (fore-hall). Then comes the *Mandapa* entry, which is symbolised in the *Sabdam*, where the interpretative part appears along with music and rhythm. When one enters the *ardha-mandapa* and the sanctum, one is in the presence of the deity. The *varnam*, the central part of a recital in which both interpretative and rhythmic dance attains full flowering, marks this moment. This is the acid test for the dancer, testing her stamina, skill and proficiency. After the *varnam*'s climax, the dancer is in intimate communion with God, the quietude of the moment signified by the *Padam*, which is purely word-based interpretation without rhythmic flashes. The *Padam* and the *Javali* are conceived in *sringar* mode. Finally, comes the *haarati* with camphor which is the *Tillana*, a blaze of rhythmic aplomb. The symbolism apart, the pure metre (*Alaripu*), the music and metre (*Jatiswaram*), the word, music and metre (*Sabdam*), and the elaboration and lofty expression of all these facets in the *varnam*, music without metre (*Padam* and *Javali*), and metre and melody in abstraction in the *Tillana* reveal the logical evolution of the dance and the pacing of the concert format. A suite of items representing each genre is called a *margam*.

With the rapid expansion of foreign rule in India in the nineteenth century, the royalty and the temple became emasculated institutions. The *devadasi*, pitted against a crumbling support system, sought individual patrons outside the temple and the court, her vulnerability exposing her to exploitation. *Tanjore Nautch* and *Dasi Attam* as *Sadir* was known, began to evoke opprobrium, the *devaradiyar* (*devadiyar*) or the *devadasi* now being solely blamed for what political and social forces had jointly contributed. The groundswell of opposition to the temple dancer grew. Led by Dr Muttulakshmi Reddy [14] in 1927, the Madras Legislative Council adopted a resolution recommending the government prepare preventive legislation against girls being initiated as *devadasis*. The same year, the Council of State at Delhi disowned the motion for prevention with the Law Department maintaining that the Indian Penal code had enough clout to deal with immoral practices. In 1930, Dr Reddy introduced a Bill in the Madras Legislative Council for prohibiting dedicatory services by *devadasis*. This was the last straw on the camel's back and would have rung

Pratibha Prahlad essays the familiar classical dance/song theme – wooing the beloved.

22

the death knell for the dance, but for a series of developments.

Amidst mounting hostility to the *devadasi* and her art form, the Indian National Congress happened to hold its annual session in 1927 in Madras (now, Chennai). An All India Music Conference was chaired by Rama Rao to coincide with this historical event. Rao was supported by two avid art lovers as secretaries: E. Krishna Iyer, a lawyer, and P. Sambamoorthi, who headed the Department of Music of Madras University. The Conference led to the inauguration of the Madras Music Academy in 1928, an institution which played a pre-eminent role in the city's cultural life. By 1930, the Quarterly Journal of the Academy became the main document of performing art events in the city, a role it fulfils to this day.

In 1932, a public function to felicitate Sri Sri Sri Raja Sir Swetachalapathi Ramakrishna Bahadur Varu Ranga Rao, Raja of Bobbili (a princely state in the Madras Presidency) on being elected leader of the Presidency Legislative Assembly, had a Sadir performance by temple dancer Sitaramudu of Bobbili. Feeling betrayed by a fellow legislator, Dr Muthulakshmi Reddy shot off protest letters to *The Hindu* and *The Mail*, at such flagrant public support for an institution the government wanted to discourage. A similar public function in honour of Muttiah Chettiar, Kumararaja of Chettinad, also included a *Sadir* performance. The English language press, *The Mail* in particular, provided ample coverage for a spirited exchange of letters.

Thanks to the self-appointed guardian of the dance, E. Krishna Iyer, who had circulated a resolution dealing with the need to encourage *Sadir*, a well-attended sixth Annual Conference of the Music Academy held in Madras discussed the 'Nautch Question' threadbare. Musical legend Tiger Varadachariyar read out a letter by G. A. Johnson, editor of *The Mail*, pleading that *Sadir* be restricted to open public platforms with 'respectable' people attending. He also pleaded for an alternative profession for the *devadasi*. The Madras opinion makers at the conference were favourable and a resolution recognising the need for public appreciation and training train dance aspirants was adopted. In 1931, the Music Academy took the bold step of presenting the Kalyani Sisters in a performance on March 15. This bid 'to expose the utter unworthiness of the criticism

that is levelled against it' (*Sadir* – Music Academy Journal) drew a scanty audience. But, the sisters, presented two years later in 1933 by the Academy, attracted a handsome turnout. In the same year, a young Balasaraswati was also presented. In an Academy Conference presided over by Vidwan K. Ponniah Pillai, Professor of Music at the Music College and descendent of Sivanandam of the Tanjore Quartet, the great Guru Meenakshi Sundaram Pillai (he was respectfully addressed as *Thata,* meaning grandfather) presented a paper on the dance and its future. The first of many efforts to educate the public had begun in earnest.[15]

The Academy re-christened *Sadir* Bharatanatyam, *Bharatam* being a prefix used for actors of the Brahmin Bhagavatulu clan. The connection with the *Natya Sastra* too must have been a consideration. While the new name was perhaps not the idea of E. Krishna Iyer alone, he was certainly instrumental in strengthening opinion that dropping *Sadir* would also help dissociate the dance from the name's negative associations in the public mind. With the freedom movement motivating a rediscovery of Indian identity, dance became a focus of interest as a great legacy of the Indian people.

Dancers from a traditional background like Gauri Amma, Balasaraswati, Varalakshmi and Saranayaki, Bhanumati, Sabharanjitam, and Nagaratnam were still performing and being presented in occasional programmes by the Music Academy, when aspirants from non-traditional backgrounds like Balachander, Lakshmi Sastri, Kalanidhi, Gopinath and Tangamani began to enter Bharatanatyam. E. Krishna Iyer himself

Dancer Yamini Krishnamurti
inspired and dominated the
Bharatanatyam scene in the
sixties and seventies; here
she conveys the power and
abandonment of love.

danced in female garb perhaps to prove that *Sadir* was a worthy art form. His initiation was under one Madhurantakam Jagadambal, a disciple of Swami Nattuvanar. What began as a casual journey to develop a basic know-how for performing the role of Malavika in Kaldiasa's play, *Malavikagnimitra*, grew into an obsession to spread the message about the art form. His vociferous support, always for the art form, was silent on the social aspect of the *devadasi*, and by encouraging youngsters particularly from Brahmin families to learn the dance, he unconsciously or knowingly separated it from the traditional practitioner. This was a point which *devadasis* like Jayamma and Nagaratnamma were not happy with and protested against.

The early thirties saw another significant entrant to the Bharatanatyam scene – Rukmini Devi, the eighth child of Nilakantha Sastry, an orthodox Brahmin. An active Theosophical Society member, she defied prevailing Brahman orthodoxy by marrying George Arundel, an Englishman who was several years her senior. In 1924, coming in contact with Russian ballerina Anna Pavlova and watching her inimitable dance of the *Dying Swan*, she became a ballet admirer and trained for the dance. Pavlova, however, urged Devi to direct herself towards rediscovering the dance of her own country. Watching traditional dancers Jeevaratnam and Varalakshmi in a recital opened her eyes, though her first encounter with Bharatanatyam at the princely state of Pudukottai – where her father was building a new palace for the ruler – had left her unmoved. With some persuasion from Krishna Iyer, an initially reluctant Guru Meenakshi Sundaram Pillai of Pandanallur agreed to teach Devi, who was all of thirty years. A quick learner, she went through what must not have been a very easy alliance for both sides. The Brahman elite of Sir C. P. Ramaswamy Iyer, T. R. Venkatarama Sastry and the Right Honourable Srinivasa Sastry pointedly boycotted her debut on the occasion of the Diamond Jubilee of the Theosophical Society in 1935 at the Adyar Theatre. It was not held in front of her Guru, who sent in his stead Subbaraya Pillai, the son of Chokkalingam Pillai, to conduct the recital, along with a relative Narasimhan for percussion support. Whatever the reason, the guru-*shishya* relationship was not all smooth sailing.

The famous dance school at Adyar, Kalakshetra,

Dancers V. P. Dhananjayan and Shanta Dhananjayan evoke an eternal theme: *Bhagwan* and *bhakta*. *Facing page:* The mother and daughter pair of Mrinalini Sarabhai and Mallika Sarabhai in the dance drama, *Mira*, choreographed by Mrinalini Sarabhai. Their institution, Darpana Academy, popularised Bharatanatyam in Ahmedabad.

set up in 1936 as the International Academy of Arts, was Rukmini Devi's brainchild. The first attempt at institutionalising Bharatanatyam training, the school established a role model for dance interwoven with education in a contemporary setting incorporating the best of the guru-*shishya* tradition. In a sylvan retreat, far from urban distractions, dance was taught in an integrated cultural setting, offering music, literature, painting, and cottage industries like weaving, all associated disciplines relevant to the dance. Being able to persuade the best dance gurus to participate in Kalakshetra – Meenakshi Sundaram Pillari, Chokkalingam Pillarim, Dandayudapani Pillai, Muthukumara Pillai, Gowri Ammal and musical giants like Tiger Varadachariyar, Mysore Vasudevachariyar, Papanasam Sivan, Budalur Krishnamurty Sastrigal – Rukmini Devi succeeded in creating a haven for art interaction at an elitist level. With her theatrical background, the dance drama understandably became the ideal medium for her sophisticated and many-sided aesthetic facility. From *Kuravanji Natakams* to *Bhagavatamela* plays, she drew upon material from traditional sources and repositioned them for the modern stage, providing her own aesthetic touch. The *Ramayanam* series was her magnum opus, the suite of six dance dramas her best[16].

Criticised in later years for not giving solo dance the importance it deserved and for 'appropriating' the *devadasi*'s art, Devi was also faulted for having over-played the devotional angle, thereby stripping Bharatanatyam of its natural, erotic exuberance – so central to it.

Considering her upbringing and that she functioned in a backdrop of animosity towards the *devadasi* and *Sadir*, both inclination and choice would have dictated the *bhakti* emphasis. The fact that a *devadasi* like Balasaraswati (the only traditional person to survive the societal onslaught) flourished as a contemporary (some attribute this to the favourable dance climate created by Devi) was proof that Devi neither intended nor posed a threat. Her example, however, certainly inspired aspirants from Brahmin families to take to Bharatanatyam.

Granddaughter of the illustrious Veenai Dhanammal and daughter of Jayammal, whose music was often described as both an audio and a visual delight for its ability to create images in the mind of

the hearer, Balasaraswati was reared in a family soaked in dance and music. She trained under guru Kandappa Pillai. The ecstasy of Bala's *sringar* depiction was as far removed from the boudoir culture the *devadasi* had come to be associated with as one could imagine. Acknowledged by Western critics and dancers too as a phenomenon, Bala, given the ordinariness of her physical persona, became the most exhilarating expression of the soaring spirit of the dance. Her *abhinaya* caught the *dhwani* or suggestive power of the word and lyric as no dance could.

A passionate debate on *Bhakti* versus *Sringar*, with Rukmini Devi and Balasaraswati representing the two, saw much bile vented on both viewpoints. But this was never a contra-indicative force in the dance, and dominance of one or the other is a matter of the dancer's aptitude and inclination.

By recruiting young boys and training them for her dance drama productions, Rukmini Devi certainly enhanced the presence of the male in what was a female-oriented dance form. The first male dancer to take Bharatanatyam to international audiences was Ram Gopal, who trained under Meenakshi Sundaram Pillai. Kalakshetra over the years created distinguished male dancers like Janardhanan, Balagopal and Dhananjayan and C. V. Chandrashekhar, who was professor and head of Department of Dance and also dean of the Faculty of Performing Arts, M. S. University, Baroda, for years. The university is one of the few that offers an academic course to qualify for a doctorate in dance. Interestingly, Bharatanatyam here began with Gurus Kannuswamy Nattuvanar and Vadivelu Pillai, son of Sivanandam Pillai of the Quartet fame with two dancers, Gowri and Sarada from Tanjore and Kumbakonam, being part of the dowry of a Tanjore princess married into the Baroda royal family.

In half a century, a sea change had overtaken the dance scene with dancers, performance spaces and audiences no longer the same. Musicians, who used to stand and follow the dancer as she moved, were nearly seated on a flank of the stage to the right of the dancer. The softer violin replaced the clarionet. Tailored costumes were introduced and even the ankle bells became a sophisticated version of the original string-tied version, being stitched on to a leather strap (leather was taboo in temples). The marathon *varnam* was reduced to half an hour. Above all, the approach to the dance was bound to change in an entirely different context, the dance now being repositioned on the proscenium by persons not born to the tradition. The gurus, after initial hiccups, had adjusted to the new environment and adapted themselves to teaching students from varied backgrounds.

The main technique of the dance, though movement changes have taken place over the years, has remained more or less the same. If an imaginary line was drawn from head to toe dividing the body into two vertical halves, the basic *araimandi* or half-seated stance with the out-turned knees of the Bharatanatyam dancer, the weight evenly distributed between the feet, it would be like drawing triangles in space. Since the joints and not the muscles dictate movement, dance lines tend to be geometrical. A grounded, highly symmetrical style, Bharatanatyam uses the jump and leap only in flashes. Leg stretches are used a great deal. Hands are moved to form straight lines and diagonals, and circling movements in space. There is an elaborate vocabulary of hand symbols used to embellish abstract movement and to represent ideas in interpretative dance, which is called *abhinaya*.

Bharatanatyam has spread all over the country beyond the wildest dreams of gurus like Muthukumara Pillai, keen to take the dance to all corners. Meenakshi Sundaram Pillai is said to have told disciples Chandrabhaga and U. S. Krishna Rao that he wanted Bharatanatyam to be known all over. With the proliferation came more versions of the dance with the Tanjavur, Pandanallur, and Vazhuvoor schools[17]. The late Kittappa Pillai always maintained that every style was only a variation in terms of emphasis of what Tanjavur propagated. He also said that Meenakshi Sundaram Pillai who gave such prominence to Pandanallur was too traditional a guru to have done anything radically different from what he was taught at Tanjavur. Mahalingam Pillai and his brother Kalyanasundaram Pillai – sons of Kuppiah Pillai, the illustrious son of famous Guru Panchapakesa Nattuvanar of Tiruvadudurai – established the famous Rarajeswari Bharatanatya Kalaalayam in Mumbai. In Karnataka, where Chinniah of the Tanjore Quartet had spent time, regional variations led to what is known as the Jetti-tayamma School, started by the daughter of a wrestler, and the Mogur School. Mrinalini Sarabhai, a disciple who trained under Meenakshi Sundaram Pillai

and Muthukumara Pillai, set up the Darpana Academy
at Ahmedabad. Gurus like K. N. Dakshinamurti,
Swaminathan and Govindarajan made their home in
Delhi.

Outside the periphery of the *sringar-bhakti* tangle,
and with the glamour of films, came young Kamala.
After her debut in 1941 under Guru Muthukumara Pillai
of Kattumannar Koil, she became a disciple of
Vazhuvoor Ramiah Pillai, the Guru and *Shishya*
representing the perfect union of two elements, each
embellishing the other. With her picture perfect
Bharatanatyam and her lighter numbers like Gypsy
Dance capturing the public imagination, the packaging
of dance for entertainment began. Earlier too, Iyer –
who had obviously thought of the crucial aspect of
entertaining motley audiences – had presented
numbers like Kite Dance and Pot Dance, where the Pot
was said to represent the universe.

After Kamala, the dancer whose fire and presence
made her a darling of the public and who became the
most sought after dancer of the sixties and seventies
in particular, was Yamini Krishnamurthy. 'Andhra by
extraction, Karnatakan by birth and Tamil by training',
Yamini was the handiwork of initial Kalakshetra training
backed by tutelage under several gurus, from each of
whom she imbibed something. An expert Kuchipudi
dancer with training in Odissi too, Yamini packaged her
performances with a little something of each dance
form. Her magnificent stage presence and aura,
unmatched rhythmic brilliance and an ability to keep
audiences spellbound; her sister Jyotishmati's singing
with father Krishnamurti introducing each item in his
grandstand English, became well known among dance
lovers. Another dancer of very different vintage
symbolising the power and grandeur of Bharatanatyam
was the far more senior Shanta Rao. A pioneer in the
post-Independence classical dance scenario, the
dancer trained under Meenakshi Sundaram Pillai.

But, proliferation has led to its own anomalies. The
imperatives of being pitch forked to the international
stage with overexposure have resulted in islands of
excellence surrounded by much mediocrity. Large
performance spaces cut out the intimacy of the dancer-
audience rapport and kill the subtleties of the dance.
In this context, interpretative dance has been the real
loser. But for the emphasis on *abhinaya* by doyenne
Kalanidhi Narayanan, the *Padam* and the *Javali*, the

really sensitive parts of a Bharatanatyam recital would have gone out of vogue. The real dialectic is between what was visualised as an inward looking art form, demanding liquidation of the dancer's ego, and the strongly individualistic contemporary dancer who has become a glamorised star, a celebrity with the media publicising her social persona rather than the dancer in her. The entire patronage system, in spite of the best efforts of the government, offers undue scope for money and proximity to power points to hog performance opportunities. The integrated approach has been fractured with the dancer depending on, but not being conversant with allied disciplines of music, and *nattuvangam*, which are specialised branches.

The young dancer of today, intelligent but impatient, often questions the logic of tradition without fully coming to grips with it. *Nayika* themes portraying woman in different situations of love, meant as a metaphor for man's eternal yearning and quest in life, are decried as exemplifying the non-liberated woman. There is a feeling that newness is what creativity is all about and when dancers regard the contemporary as a present totally unrelated to the past, instead of evolving from it, there is a rudderlessness which makes experimental work often clueless. Instead of being creatively imitative, dancers search for ways of being different from what is regarded as a much-worn repertoire. There is a clear polarisation on the question of how Bharatanatyam should respond to the contemporary context. For many senior dancers like Leela Samson and Malavika Sarukkai, working within the tradition offers enough space for fresh ideas, within the prescribed classical format. Says Bharatanatyam dancer Alarmel Valli: 'As a point in the continuum of time, I am contemporary, and not a museum relic; neither is my art which brings such joy to me and the audiences.' V. P. Dhananjayan asserts that he has been able to interact with ballet dancers in *Jungle Boy*, jointly presented by his institution Bharata Kalangali and the Ohio Ballet Dance Company, without distorting Bharatanatyam.

While there are cries for divesting the dance of its connection with myth, the conviction that spirituality and not religiosity is the aim of Bharatanatyam is also strongly voiced. Taking on the Bharatanatyam establishment with her individualistic approach, by focusing on the dancer's body and spine, by using Yoga

Dancer Leela Samson traces a perfect diagonal movement in *nritta*.
Facing page: The joy and exultation of total surrender – Alarmel Valli.

and martial art traditions as reinforcing links is the dancer, Chandralekha. Her latest productions, however, have little to do with the Bharatanatyam body language (though they may well be inspired by it) or music.

Lowering standards and ill-informed audiences cannot become arguments against a dance form.

The female dancer is still preferred by audiences, and even for talented male dancers performance opportunities are too few. The search for new spaces in an art form is part of a continuing journey and there cannot be any formula for original work. Bharatanatyam today is seen in myriad manifestations. In the West, the large Indian diaspora is working at different levels to make the dance relate to an alien context where it is clubbed under either 'ethnic' or 'South Asian art.' The compulsions in the West are producing different manifestations of the dance.

In a hectic dance scene, the tension between the old and the new will go on and one cannot see either rooting out the other. As Lakshmi Viswanathan once remarked, 'Of course, we cannot be and are not what the *devadasi* was. But that is the hardy nature of Bharatanatyam: it has survived the upheavals of history, reinventing itself in different ages.'

Her Voice, a production on the theme of women and peace, involved dancing and puppetry; the choreographer was Geeta Chandran, the puppeteer Anurupa Roy.
Following page 40: A character being introduced from behind the curtain in the Kuravanji style. In this performance, Padma Subramaniam, Chitra Visweswaran, and Sudharani Raghupati took the three main roles.
Following page 41: Spanda, choreographed by Leela Samson.
Following page 42: Prerana Shrimali, one of the best Jaipur *gharana* specialists.

Kathak

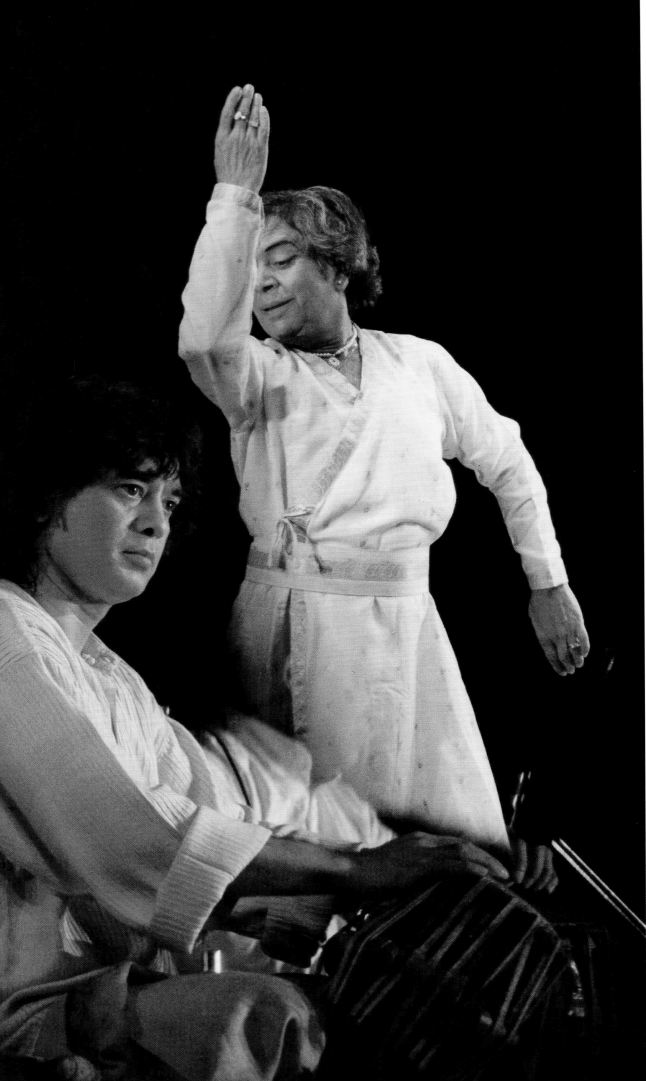

'If my father (Achhan Maharaj) were to see the dance today, I doubt he would recognise some of it as Kathak.' Was Birju Maharaj's remark a compliment to the changes seen in the Kathak scene of the last fifty years, or was it a veiled regret about dilution of classical depth? Perhaps, a little of both!

The term Kathak etymologically derived from *Katha* or story, stands for a class or community of storytellers referred to as Gaur Brahmins. Like our ancient bards and minstrels regaling audiences through dramatised narrations from mythology using poetry, the spoken word, music, mime and rhythm, simultaneously entertaining, informing and sermonising, narrative traditions like the *Harikatha* in the south, and what continues in the temples of Ayodhya and Uttar Pradesh, have helped weld communities. The word *Kathaka* in the *Mahabharata* and the *Ramayana* refers to rhapsodists like Kusilava narrating the story of Rama. Sanskrit literature has references to *Grantikas* and *Pathakas*. In time, Kathak came to stand for the stylised dance form believed to have evolved out of the vocabulary of the storyteller's art, though conclusive evidence on the *Kathak-Kathakar* connection needs more research. Nineteenth-century Census records mention Kathaks living in and around Benares, Azamgarh, Rae Bareilly, Pratapgarh, and Gorakhpur.

Nurtured in areas roughly pertaining to present-day Uttar Pradesh, Madhya Pradesh and Rajasthan, Kathak is the only Indian dance style combining both Hindu and Islamic influences, one giving it the myth and the other its brilliant virtuosity and secular aspect. It is also the only Indian classical form with a vast body of abstract dance, enabling entire recitals to be sustained on the rhythmic content alone without interpretative dance built on a word-based text. Another distinguishing feature is the upright stance, the body of the dancer held absolutely erect, without the knee deflections or the half-seated position with out-turned knees common to Indian dance forms. This posture was a post-seventeenth century development, for whatever remains of fourteenth-fifteenth century temple architecture in Rajasthan and Uttar Pradesh shows the dancer in the *ardhamandali* (half-seated position) common to Bharatanatyam. Even sixteenth century Jain and Rajasthani paintings and miniatures of women playing the *mardala* or cymbals do not show them in the erect posture. Pictures of Krishna in a half skirt worn over leggings have, till the late-seventeenth century, flexed knees. By the sixteenth century, pictures of women clad in transparent full skirts or *lehengas*, revealing the *chudidars* underneath, show feet with ankle bells[1].

Fifteenth-century Sanskrit texts on music mention dance. Courtesans and later the somewhat infamous Nautch Girls of the Raj, played a role in preserving Kathak. But the dance in its vintage classical manifestation is attributed to male dancers/gurus. While not eschewing the Siva myth, it is the Krishna emphasis of the Bhakti movement, which provided the dance its thematic thrust. The *Ras Lila* of Brindavan, the *Ashtachap* poets[2], the songs of Meera and of Swami Haridas reveal dance as a familiar poetic motif. They contain *Bols*, mnemonic syllables and terms, part of the Kathak vocabulary today. Though not exactly like the Devadasi tradition, the Devasthanam Records of Rajasthan do mention women attached to the Govind Deo temple for singing and dancing[3].

Not surprisingly, the Hindu myth had little interest for the Islamic rulers whose main contribution came through music. Allauddin Khilji, the Sultan of Delhi (1296-1316) commissioned Nayak Gopal to translate Dhrupad compositions in Sanskrit into the spoken Braj Bhasha. By the time of Amir Khusro, during mid-thirteenth to fourteenth centuries, Indian *raga* music had influenced Persian music. Hindu and Muslim musicians codified details of *Dhrupad* in *Man Kutuhal* at the time of Raja Man Singh Tomar of Gwalior (1486-1518). The *Khayal* as a genre became famous. The first Persian book on Indian music, *Lahjat-e-Sikandar Shahi*, also appeared and *Kitab-e-Nauras*, composed during the reign of Ibrahim Adil Shah 11, Sultan of Bijapur (1580-1626), had songs on Hindu deities. To quote the popular saying, 'The Lotus had met the Rose.'

While dance could not remain uninfluenced by the *Dhrupad* and *Khayal*, neither of these genres has the structured textual format easy for translation into dance. The improvisatory open-ended approach in the music acquired a rhythmic dimension in dance. Far more suitable for kinetic and mimetic interpretation were the *Bhajan* and the *Ghazal*, one devotional and the other poetic. What emerged as the ideal musical base for interpretative dance was the *Thumri*. The *Khayal* with its unchartered improvised canvas demands lofty musical creativity, while the *Thumri* with a romantic thrust and more optimistic tone than the sensuous, pain-

filled *Ghazal*, lends itself to dance interpretation. The *bais* and courtesans, great singers, explored the coquetry and suggestive undertones of the lyrics. These, quite contrary to the male viewpoint in the *ghazal*, represented *sringar* from the female perspective.

By the close of the eighteenth century, the declining Mughal court saw vassals setting themselves up as independent rulers. Musicians and dancers confronting uncertain court patronage had begun filtering to the Awadh area where Nawab Asaf-Ud-Daulah, a known art lover ruled from 1775-1798. Under Nawab Wajid Ali Shah (1847-1856) Kathak had its richest flowering with the *Thumri-Kathak* connection reaching new heights, the ruler being a fond dancer and musician. The Lucknow School of Kathak, as it came to be known later, began to acquire an identity. A flamboyant man given to indulgence, Wajid Ali Shah constructed the grand Kaiser Baug and a special *Parion Ka Khana*, where courtesans and dancers were trained. The Nawab composed *Rahas*, a Kathak ballet with the ruler in the main role. Based on Syed Agha Hassan Amanat's *Indersabha*, conceived on the Sanskrit model of *Vikramorvashiyam*, a sumptuous musical opera-cum-dance production featuring all the famous *paris* became a public favourite. The Nawab himself wrote works like *Banni* and *Najo* and *Gunch-e-Raga* and *Saut-ul-Mubarak* describing the *Gat*, an aspect of Kathak he specialised in. Durga Prasad and Thakur Prasad, sons of Prakashji who had been part of the court of Asaf-ud-daula, became famous at Wajid Ali Shah's court, the former teaching the Nawab. Durga Prasad's sons Kalka and Bindadin and the three sons of Kalka Maharaj – Achhan Maharaj, Lachhu Maharaj and Shambhu Maharaj – are the main architects of present-day Kathak of the Lucknow School, the *gharana* having its most charismatic teacher/performer today in Pandit Birju Maharaj, son of Achhan Maharaj.

The court maintained special teachers to train the harem women and interested begums of the Sultan. Too lost in the arts to govern, Wajid Ali Shah was finally deported and pensioned off by the East India Company to spend his last days in Kolkata.

Meanwhile, different Kathak streams had evolved in the princely states of Rajasthan in and around Bikaner, in Jaipur, Udaipur, and Amber. Old miniatures and Rajasthani paintings testify to the old dance connection. The dancers of Rajasthan under the patronage of Hindu rulers, unlike their Lucknow counterparts, had no compulsion to dilute the emphasis on myth. Records mention *Kathaks* living around Churu, Sujangarh, Shekhawati and other places. The earliest known dancer, Bhanuji, was a reputed Siva devotee, and Jaipur *gharana's Kavit* compositions reflect Saivite reverence, though Rajasthan art on the whole carries Saiva, Sakta, and Vaishnavite preferences. Rulers like Maharaja Sawai Jai Singh of Amber (1699-1743) and his successors were avid Vishnu worshippers. Treatises of music were written in the spoken language of Rajasthani or a dialect of Hindi, and not Sanskrit, as art was more than just an elitist concern. Courtesans as reputed singers and dancers were part of court culture. Special to what later came to be known as the Jaipur School of Kathak was the Gunijankhana, an institution, started by Sawai Jai Singh. It gave succour to artistes and gurus who could concentrate on creative work without livelihood worries. Encouraging artist interaction, the Gunijankhana continued to flourish under Sawai Pratap Singh (1778-1803) and succeeding rulers. With dwindling princely power, the shrinking protective umbrella made many artistes migrate. Unlike the Lucknow *Gharana* where lineage is traced from one main line, with activity centred in Lucknow and nearby areas, the Jaipur School had several artist families, travelling and settling down in several parts of the country, making tracing of links in the Kathak chain more complicated. Each court maintained its own artistes, and different Kathak families while interconnected, invested the art with distinct characteristics, the multiplicity of styles often leading to confusing rivalries. About fifty years ago, representatives of the many streams met and decided to unite under the name, Jaipur *Gharana*, a safeguard against the many lean Kathak tributaries disintegrating into nothingness in the larger Kathak scene. The choice of name was prompted by the political stature of the state rather than any special artistic claims.

In the male-dominated martial culture of Rajasthan, the *Thumri* with its feminine delicacy did not find a conducive artistic atmosphere for dance elaboration as in the Lucknow school, even though the *sringar* emphasis in the songs of Meera, who defied aristocratic conventions, is frankly sensual. Jaipur gurus like Narayan

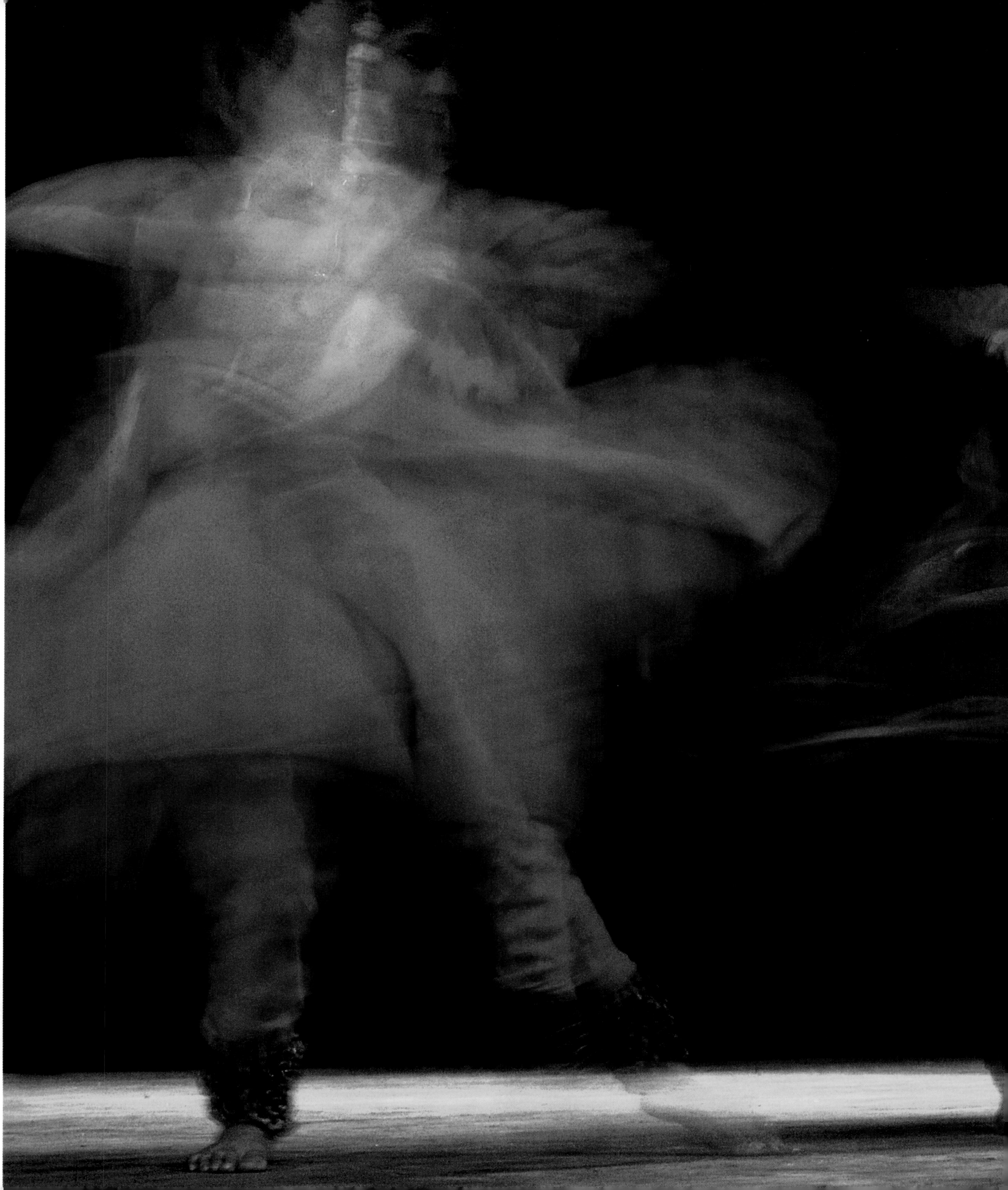

The *chakkar* or pirouette has stunning visual appeal. *Preceding page 44:* Two maestros, Pandit Birju Maharaj, Kathak's most well-known name, with Ustad Zakir Hussein on the *tabla*. *Preceding page 45:* Uma Sharma's *ghagra* (skirt) swirls during a graceful *gat*. *Preceding page 46:* Rajendra Gangani covers the floor with crossed feet. *Preceding page 47:* Front, back or sideways, the body speaks as Pandit Birju Maharaj explores Kathak's rich tapestry of forms.

Prasad's brothers Mohan Lal and Chiranji Lal were *Thumri* singers, the popular *Aaj maika kunwar kaan Barje*, being Mohan Lal's own composition.

Gharana claims and counterclaims are part of the Kathak story. Guru Sunderprasad, one of the bywords for Jaipur Kathak, is said to have learnt under the Lucknow *Thumri* King, Bindadin. In Mumbai, Guru Sunderprasad later started the Bindadin School of Kathak, training students who became famous names in Kathak – Mohanrao Kalyanpurkar, Madame Menaka, Sohan Lal, Roshan Kumari and others. Jaipur *gharana* specialists deny the Guru ever learnt under Bindadin while acknowledging his deep admiration for the Lucknow Guru. His *bandishes*, they say, never reflected any Lucknow *gharana* influence nor did his teaching betray any signs of this training, if indeed it was true. 'Many of the compositions now ascribed to Maharaj Bindadin, no doubt a great guru, were a later reassembling of scattered segments with inputs from more than one source,' says a Jaipur *gharana* exponent. When Guru Sunderprasad moved over to Delhi to teach at the Bharatiya Kala Kendra in 1958, dancers like Uma Sharma, Urmila Nagar, Kumudini Lakhia and the late Durga Lal trained under him. Teachers like Mohanrao Kalyanpurkar, who trained in both *gharanas* and later taught students like Durga Lal, recognised as Jaipur *gharana* stalwarts, kept the two inheritances separately identified in his dance. With many dancers opting to learn from gurus of both schools (a point that government scholarships also insist on), *gharana* distinctions have become irrelevant and blurred today, though the desire to preserve distinctive identities persists among traditional families.

One Janakiprasad from Bikaner from the Jaipur *gharana* strain settled down in Benares which had a flourishing *tawaif* culture and there began yet another line of Kathak named after him – sometimes also referred to as the Benares *Gharana*. Janakiprasad had no issue, though successors from this line, Hazarilal (trained by Ashiq Hussain Khan) and his wife Sunayana, settled in Mumbai. Another reputed dancer Krishna Kumar was brought to Delhi by Nirmala Joshi, who along with art-minded persons like Dr Kapila Vatsyayan transformed the art climate of Delhi.

The former princely state of Raigarh in Madhya Pradesh was ruled by art patrons, and dancers from other states frequented the court. But there was no

Five beguiling *nayikas*: (clockwise from bottom left) Gitanjali Lal, Prerana Shrimali, Rani Karna, Nandini Singh, and Saswati Sen.

52

The world becomes dizzy
with dance as Saswati Sen
executes a pirouette.

history of a Kathak tradition till Raja Chakradhar Singh who came to rule in 1935 gave a new dimension to the dance scene through his own compositions. A *tablist* and *Pakhawaj* player of no mean merit, and scholar and composer to boot, Chakradhar Singh compiled massive treatises like *Nartan Sarwaswam* and *Tala-toyanidhi*, on the dance and metrical cycles or *talas*. *Paran* compositions like *Kadak-Bijli, Chamak Bijli, Dal-Badal* and many others reveal the composer's uncanny ear for piling sound atop sound in an onomatopoeic arrangement, the rhythmic syllables he used typical of the thematic image of each composition. The large repertoire and intricate diagrams of *tala* cycles form the Raigarh heritage. Picking candidates from humble peasant, washermen and rickshaw-pulling families, Chakradhar Singh arranged for their professional training under stalwarts from the Lucknow and the Jaipur *gharanas*, the dance consequently reflecting the influence of both schools. Kartik Ram, Kalyan Mahant and Firturam Vaishnav became famous, Kartik Ram and Kalyan blossoming as a twosome winning every state-level competition. A request from the Nawab of Rampur for the two dancers to grace his court for a spell is said to have provoked the response, 'Take half my kingdom instead!' [4] With the declining powers of royalty, the dancers began reverting to their hereditary professions. Then, an enterprising Madhya Pradesh bureaucrat in 1980[5] began the Chakradhar Singh Nritya Kendra and Kartik Ram was summoned from his village to teach. Half a dozen disciples are undergoing training under Kartik Ram's son Ram Lal in this institution. The rhythmic aspect is Jaipur in style, and the *abhinaya* part shows the Lucknow influence.

The Nawabi ambience bestowed *nazaquat* and refinement on the Lucknow school. Its repertoire of *Thumris* carries the subtle eroticism of the *tawaif* and the courtesan culture. The Jaipur school, on the other hand, prides itself on its brilliant *layakari*: its long *Parans*, the one-legged *chakkars* or pirouettes (*Eka Pada Bhramaris*), *Kavits* and also *Sangeet Ka Tukras* like 'Drig Jagira Drig Jagira' and 'Tawa Thungataka'. Unlike the practice of fitting teen *tala* rhythmic *bandishes* into other *talas* by a slight re-spacing of the rhythmic syllables, the Jaipur *gharana* insists on compositions distinct to each *tala*. While this *gharana* is rich in its compositions for each *tala*, the Lucknow *gharana* has greater presentational sophistication. Though less

evident today, the Jaipur school is credited with immense ability for sustaining long dance spells in the *vilambit laya* (slow pace).

The Janakiprasad *gharana* specialises in *Bols* outside the scope of either the *tabla* or the *Pakhawaj* and these *Naach Bols* form one of its stylistic features.

The Lucknow *gharana* too owes its prominence to a long line of charismatic performer-gurus who have left behind a strong line of disciples. Sons of the exceptionally talented Bindadin and Kalka Maharaj have left an indelible mark on Kathak – Achhan Maharaj by the measured grace, and refinement of line and rhythm, and Shambhu Maharaj by taking Kathak *abhinaya* to its zenith of abstraction and suggestive richness. His interpretation of *thumris* like 'Bata do Guinyan, Kaun galin gayo Shyam' and 'Baithe Soche Brijbhama' have remained unparalleled examples of what levels expressional dance can aspire to. Settling down in Mumbai as a dance composer for films was Lachhu Maharaj, the master of *lasya anga* or graceful movements, with a unique genius for weaving emotive images out of pure rhythmic numbers. He was commissioned to choreograph the first dance drama, *Malati Madhav*, based on Bhavabhuti's classic, produced in 1958 by the Bharatiya Kala Kendra. Nephew Birju Maharaj, who has absorbed the best from each of the brothers, adding to it his own creative genius and performance appeal, keeps the Lucknow flag flying high. Among his innumerable students are Saswati Sen, and Krishan Mohan and Ram Mohan, sons of Guru Shambhu Maharaj. The great gurus of Jaipur Kathak belonged less to the performer class that captured capturing public imagination. Teachers have rarely transmitted their specialised skills even to the most talented students. Charismatic dancers Devi Lal and Durga Lal unfortunately died young. One of the Jaipur *gharana* specialists, Prerana Shrimali, recalls how Sunderprasad's feat of dancing on a *Gulal* heap, spreading the colour with his flat-footed rhythmic tapping into a perfectly etched figure of an elephant, was not taught even to his best students. Guru Gaurishankar – who danced with Madame Menaka, one of the first to tour countries like China with her troupe – demonstrated in a Kathak Kendra festival in 1978 an intriguing circling movement, *Agrapheri Ka Kavach palta*, which he did not even teach his own son. 'Most of the dance composing for the famous film *Pakeeza*, barring 'Thade rahiyo Bankhe'

composed by Lachhu Maharaj, was his work[6].' Closer to our own times, neither Charan Giridhar Chand nor the late Tej Prakash Tulsi, sons of the reputed Narayan Prasad, acquired even a whiff of the father's brilliant and inimitable '*Nav-Ki-Gat*'.

Kathak like Bharatanatyam reached a low point when only the *Nautch* figured as a visible remnant of the dance. When American dancers Ruth St. Denis and Ted Shawn and Russian ballerina Pavlova came to India, what they were treated to was Kathak by the *tawaif* Bachwa Jan at Kolkata. The good dancers remained confined to the courts.

The first woman to defy social stigma attached to the dance was Madame Menaka who had trained under Pandit Sitaram Misra, Ram Dutt and Lachhu Maharaj. The forties, a period of rediscovery for dance, saw Achhan Maharaj invited to teach at Bharatiya Sangeet Sadan with the likes of Nirmala Joshi and Dr Kapila Vatsyayan becoming his disciples. Communal tension and the sudden demise of Achhan Maharaj in 1947 disrupted the movement, till Shambhu Maharaj, in 1952, became a part of the Bharatiya Kala Kendra with Kathak as its main activity. Teenaged Birju Maharaj commissioned to teach at Bharatiya Sangeet Sadan, after a while, came over to the Bharatiya Kala Kendra. When the Kathak wing became an independent institution directly under the Sangeet Natak Akademi in 1964, he headed its faculty for years before he retired, becoming director for a stint. His multi-sided talents as teacher, dancer, composer, singer and percussionist undoubtedly enhanced the Lucknow *gharana*.

Stylistically, Kathak is less concerned with covering floor space than creating a soundscape of tonal variations, through its footwork and ankle bell sounds. In no other dance does tapping the floor with flat feet acquire the aural dimension it does in Kathak. This ability to weave intricate rhythmic combinations into the metrical cycle or *tala* is called *Tattakara*. To quote S. K. Saxena's observations[7], this part gives *aakaar* or form to *tat* or essence and is essentially an exploration of the *tala*, with the feet, indeed the entire body, becoming a percussion instrument. Hence the observation, that the Kathak dancer 'dances a *tala*' rather than 'to a *tala*'. While appearing to be static, the dancer with a constant but subtle manipulation of weight produces tonal variations and shifting accents in rhythmic patterns. Another stylistic feature is the pirouette (*bhramari*) rendered with one foot anchored to the floor while the other like a compass needle tracing a circle provides bodily thrust for the movement. All abstract dance is performed to a repetitive musical refrain called *Nagma*[8] or *Lehra*, played on the *sarangi*. The dancer's upper torso, through a delicate shoulder inclined towards one side, imparts to movement and posture a fluid grace. These infinitesimal torso and wrist movements are known as *kasak masak*. The torso in the Jaipur style is held in a more sedate frontal position.

The *nritta* or abstract non-interpretative part of a Kathak recital comprises brief units, each complete yet part of an interwoven wider canvas, which is why Dr S. K. Saxena prefers to refer to the units as 'intra-forms'. Rhythm, as the measurement of time, places emphasis on the *sama*, the first beat of the *tala*, representing both the 'coming home' after the completion of a rhythmic cycle, and the starting point of another. The dancer's entry in a rhythmic flash is *Amad*, followed by *Thaat*, in which the body slowly awakens to the rhythmic impulses stirred by the *Lehra*, culminating in gentle freezes on the *sama*, the postures in varied profile bringing out the beauty of micro movements. A dancer recollects[9] how her guru Kundanlal Gangani would ask her to execute *Thata* sequences on a muslin cloth spread on the floor, insisting that movement and *chal* be so infinitesimally delicate that on completing the sequence the cloth stay unwrinkled. The zigzagging feet rubbing on the floor as the dancer moves sideways is again typical of the Jaipur school. Full-blown rhythmic articulation comes with the *Tukras* and *Toras* based on the mnemonics of the *tabla* and the *Paran*, based on the heavy aspirated mnemonics of the *Pakhawaj*. The dancer after each sequence may revert to foot-tapping rhythmics as the anchoring point and link between units. *Tihais*, crisp rhythmic arrangements repeated thrice, are a feature of the footwork. *Parmelu* is a composition combining mnemonics of a variety of percussion instruments. A graceful part of the dance is *Gat Nikas* or *Gat Bhav*, performed to the *lehra*, without a word of content, where the dancer presents cameos from life such as the gait of different animals or a woman sending out discrete messages by manipulating her veil. Even little episodes from myths like *Makkhan Chor* (butter thief Krishna) are presented with *abhinaya*, which rests on its own here without the sung word. *Dadras, Bhajans,* and *Thumris* provide textual material for interpretative

dance. The *Tarana*, regarded as the forerunner of the Bharatanatyam *Tillana*, is based on rhythmic syllables set to a melodic mode. This often forms the concluding abstract dance statement in a recital.

Kathak has proliferated, spreading to the globe through the Indian diaspora. Commanding the best of teachers, government training institutions have created countless competent, but few inspiring dancers. The proscenium distance between performer and audience has resulted in erasing the subtleties of an eyebrow or wrist movement or torso genuflection. The story goes that a visitor to the Nawab's reception, seeing the corpulent Achhan Maharaj casually replacing the end of his shawl on the shoulder, concluded that he was seeing a dancer in action. Contrarily, today's mixed and not particularly well-informed audience mistakes cleverly rehearsed rhythmic razzmatazz for improvised brilliance. Delicate aspects like *Thaat* and *Gat* have become minimal in the vertigo of speed and virtuosity that have taken over. Days when the ability to sustain *vilambit* spells was priced are gone. *Thumri* singing for *Kathak* has become like *Ghazal* singing, and barring exceptions like Rohini Bhate who insists on music of the highest classicism for dance, Kathak music rarely rises above perfunctory levels. The *Nagma* that should reflect not just *tala* beats, but its cadence and emphasis, has become a mechanical refrain. The dancer's lessening connections with poetry and literature have diminished fresh interpretative or thematic insights and *abhinaya* is the loser. Dancers like Uma Sharma, still hung on the Shambhu Maharaj magic of *abhinaya*, tend to be regarded as anachronisms, and love poetry interpreted in dance is often reduced to coquettish portrayals.

Helping to accommodate too many dancers jostling for performance space is the dance drama genre, which has proliferated. From Wajid Ali Shah's *Rahas* to Madame Menaka's group efforts and from a duet of Sitara Devi and Pandit Birju Maharaj to Bharatiya Kala Kendra's *Malati Madhav* was a great stride. It started a trend which had come to stay and received enthusiastic support from choreographers and audiences.

For a sophisticated exploring of the Kathak form for group possibilities, the credit goes to dancer-choreographer Kumudini Lakhia, Shambhu Maharaj's student whose earlier association with Ram Gopal as a troupe member had opened her eyes to movements in space-time. The first to deconstruct Kathak movements

into micro-units, reassembling them for group geometry, Kumudini disassociated the dance from the conventional Krishna focus by harnessing its potential for many themes. Fussy frills, veils, and jewellery were substituted by simple elegance in costuming, putting the emphasis on the dance lines of more than a solo dancer performing in relation to other dancers. Finding a like-minded musician in Atul Desai, she began a long artistic collaboration, creating pathbreaking productions: *Dhabkar*, *Atah Kim*, *Duvidha*, *The Peg*, and *Okha Haran*.

Kathak Kendra's annual Bindadin Mahotsava, started by the then Kendra director, Keshav Kothari, has provided a pan-Indian platform for Kathak interaction and also led to competing creative efforts. From games like *Gullidanda* and *Kho Kho* to tales of missing files in dusty offices, conceived and produced by Birju Maharaj, the dance form has been harnessed to a plethora of themes. Interactions with the Spanish Flamenco[10] and Hip Hop dancers, and *Jugalbandis* have become fashionable. After Daksha Seth's experiment in exploring the *Kathak Chakkar*, adapting it to Vivaldi's music decades ago, many lesser experiments with Western music have been tried. Inspired by other narrative forms, a production like *Ram Katha Ram Kahani* was done by Chetna Jalan in Padatik. But freewheeling disasters have also dotted the scene, ringing alarm bells about where the dance is headed. Questions are being asked about the best direction 'otherness' should take so that the dance does not lose its intrinsic identity, its improvisatory spark and open-ended approach within its grammar and form. There is a lot of activity but not often does one see work beyond the level of mechanical sameness with so many dancers, all wanting to shine in solo glory rather than be part of an ensemble. There are not enough platforms. But, in the mixed scene, there are worthy dancers who shine as an example what classicism means. What is being seen is a phase in the flow of dance through time – one of adjustments to globalisation and its compulsions.

Birju Maharaj, perhaps the greatest of teachers Kathak has produced, sums up the results of market forces and a giddy performance scene, where the urge to be different is yet to be backed by sufficient ideational scaffolding. 'Few students come to me to learn the dance,' he says. 'What they want to learn are "items" for the performance.' But the scene will change.

57

Two glimpses of group
Kathak: *(top)* Kumudini
Lakhia's innovative
production performed by
Kadamb students; *(bottom)*
Surya Jyoti by Luna Poddar
and her troupe during
Kalashram's Kathak Festival.
Facing page: Shovana
Narayan displays the
abhinaya of ecstasy.
Following pages 58-59:
Prerana Shrimali: the *nayika*
in a myriad moods as she
interprets a Begum Akhtar
ghazal.

Odissi

'Those with some sense of shame play musical instruments, and those with none sing. As for the utterly shameless, they take to dancing.'

Compare this saying in the Orissa of the nineteenth and early twentieth centuries with the last fifty years of Odissi, the period during which the dance has risen like the Phoenix from being a skeletal remnant of history to reincarnate as one of the most sought after classical forms – and one has a remarkable instance of cultural recovery in art history. What is seen as traditional Odissi today is a superstructure crafted but fifty years ago, erected on the foundation of lean pickings. Even in the early forties, a traditional dance recital was an uninterrupted ten-to-fifteen-minute sequence comprising elementary movement and music. The restructuring was the work of scholars and dance practitioners, the latter men of humble origin not born to any dance tradition as such, but who through talent, powers of acute observation and assimilation, and unstinting effort revitalised the art form - evolving into gurus in the truest sense of the term. What was in most dances a journey from temple and court to the proscenium, became here a movement of the disintegrating dance finding a foothold in theatre, where the first seeds of the new dance were sown.

The historicity of Odissi is irrefutable, for even the *Natya Sastra* mentions 'Odra Magadhi' as one of the four regional dances[1]. Scholars have identified Odra Magadhi as the Vanga, Kalinga, Anga, Odra, Magadha and Pundra regions, of which Kalinga and Odra refer to present-day Orissa. The name Orissa (also Utkala and Kalingadesa) is believed to be a corruption of the Sanskrit term *Odra Desha*. The *Odras* were the region's earliest Aryan settlers who had overpowered the Kalingas and Dravidas, but were in turn subjugated by the Utkalas.

The Chedi, Sailodbhava, Bhaumakara, Soma Vamsi, Ganga and Gajapati dynasties, and Jainism, Buddhism, Hinduism, Tantrism as well as tribal religions have contributed vital strands to Orissa's cultural history.

The earliest architectural evidence of dance in India is found in the first-century B.C. rock-cut caves of Udayagiri near Bhubaneswar, where in an edict in the Hatigumpha cave, Jain emperor Kharavela refers to himself as *Gandharva-Veda-Buddha*, an expert in dance, drama and music, Gandharva being a synonym for the arts. Carved figures of flying celestial dancers apart, there

63

Lord Jagannath is a powerful presence on the Odissi stage; the dancer, here the late Sanjukta Panigrahi, offers her art to him.
Facing page: (top) Sharon Lowen, woman with a lamp; (bottom) Jyoti Srivastava, looking through the window, *Preceding page 60:* The dancing feet of Madhavi Mudgal.

is a group sequence of men and women performing round a Chaita tree accompanied by musicians. The post-Kharavela, early Buddhist phase is a less-known page of Orissan history, till Mahayana Buddhism and Tantrism from the sixth century A.D. onwards find architectural expression in the Lalitagiri and Ratnagiri *viharas* and allied monuments with elaborately carved dancing gods, goddesses, and couples. The sixth-century Kosaleswara temple in Bolangir has the earliest representation of a figure in *Tribhanga*[2], and the seventh-century Parasuramesvara temple in Bhubaneswar has a strongly sculpted figure in Chauka – both main stylistic concerns of Odissi. The Kapileswar temple has male dancing figures on the walls. An abundance of Nataraja figures adorn the sixth-seventh century Bharateswar, Lakshmaneswar and Satrughneswar temples, so too at Bhubaneswar. And the earliest known Nataraja figure attributed to the fourth century is from Asanpat in Orissa. The region centred round Bhubaneswar formed a strong Saivite belt, the best-known symbol of the Siva emphasis being the Lingaraj Temple, full of dancing figures. Begun by Yayatikesari, it was completed by his successors in the middle of the eleventh century. In the jewel-like Mukteswar and Rajarani temples are exquisite figures of *alasyakanyas*[3], the pose prominent in Odissi. While Lord Jagannath at Puri became the centre of the *mahari* or *devadasi*, the most magnificent architectural statement of the dancer remains the Konarak temple, dedicated to Surya, the Sun God. It was built by the Ganga emperor, Narasingha Deva I (1238-1264), with a special *Natya Mandap* (*nata-mandir*) replete with life-size figures of dancers and instrumentalists – all inspiration for Odissi choreography[4].

Inscriptional evidence of women dedicated to temple service is found in the eleventh-century Brahmeswara temple (1060), built by Kolavati Devi, queen of Yayati Kesari, the builder of the Lingaraj temple, and mother of Udyotakesari of the Soma dynasty. The foundation inscription of the Anantavasudeva temple[5], preserved in the London Museum, describes the builder of the temple Chandrika, daughter of Anangabhina Deva III (1211-1238) as learned in song and dance – 'gitagnya, layatala nartanakala kaushalya'.

Marital alliances confirm extensive contacts between the south and the east. A Chola inscription records the marriage of Rajasundari, the daughter of Kulottunga Chola I to Rajaraja IV, an Eastern Ganga King

Guru Kelucharan Mohapatra, the doyen of Odissi, performs an interpretative item in his exquisite manner.

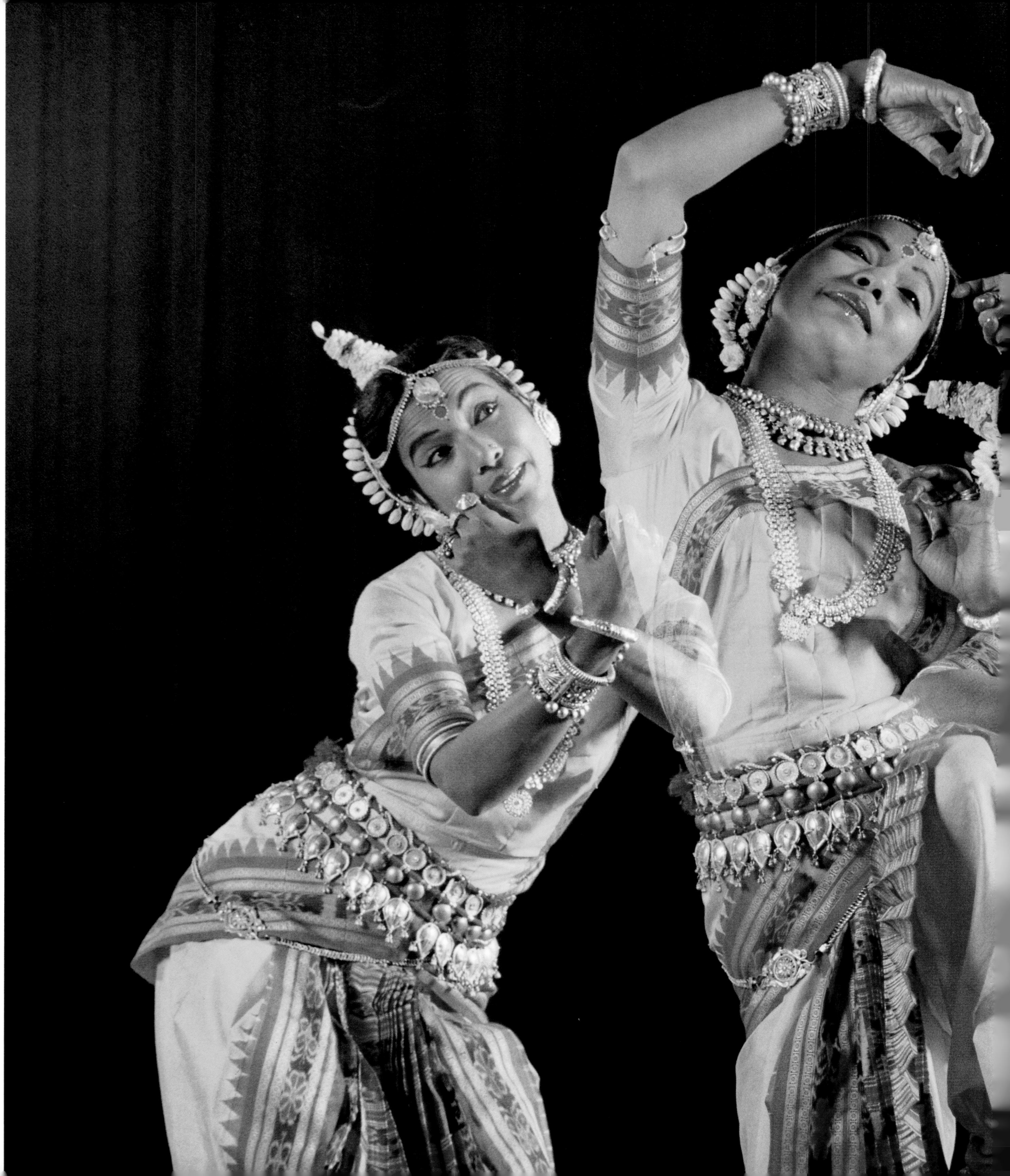

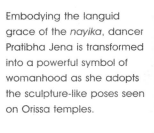

Embodying the languid grace of the *nayika*, dancer Pratibha Jena is transformed into a powerful symbol of womanhood as she adopts the sculpture-like poses seen on Orissa temples.

ruling over the Kalinga region, and mentions dancers and musicians accompanying the princess as part of the dowry. Out of the Chola-Ganga wedlock was born Anantavarma Chodaganga (1076-1147) who settled the dancers of the *Telinga Sampradaya*[6] in Chudanga or the Choda Ganga *sahi* (street) of Puri. A Saivite, Anantavarma Choda Ganga turned into a devout Vaishnavite, his highest tribute to God being the Jagannath temple of Puri, emerging as the focal point for the *Vaishnavite Mahari* or temple dancer of Orissa.

An inscription in Oriya by Prataparudra Deva, a Gajapati ruler, dated 1499 and engraved in the Jagannath temple, orders the *Telinga Sampradaya* and the Oriya dancing girls to render verses only from the *Gita Govind*[7] from *bhoga* (early morning) to *Bada Singara* (bed-time) for *Bada Thakur* (Balaram) and *Gita Govind Thakur* (Jagannath). The dance during the *bhoga* was rhythmic while during the *Bada Singar* it was *abhinaya*[8] oriented. Four Vaishnavite singers sang *Gita Govind* verses. The order concludes with the proclamation that any superintendent knowingly allowing any other song to be sung would incur the wrath of Jagannath.

One Padmavati, a *devadasi*, is believed to have become the wife of *natyacharya* and poet, Jayadeva, whose immortal *Gita Govind* forms one of the staples for interpretative dance in Odissi. Regarded as the 'son of the soil' by Oriyas and Bengalis, this poet with his Vaishnavite ardour influenced all of eastern, northeastern and southern Indian art. His Radha Madhava cult had a long history in Orissa, with Madhava temples from the seventh to twelfth centuries found round Kenduli village, regarded as the birth place of Jayadeva.

Puri Jagannath, a Vaishnavite centre, drew saints like Chaitanya Mahaprabhu and his ardent follower, the Governor of Rajamundry (Rajamahendrapuram), Ramananda Patnaik. He is said to have taught *abhinaya* to *maharis* and even had them enact *Gita Govind*.

Initiated with a piece of cloth from the Jagannath idol being tied round her head (the *Saree Bandha* ceremony), the *Mahari* was regarded as wed to the Lord, and could no longer partake of home-cooked food. Nor could she look at the audience while dancing, for in the *Sakta* and *Tantric* approach common to Orissa, the temple woman symbolised *sakti* and procreation.

Belonging to different categories, the *Nachuni* (female dancer), *Bhitar Gauni* (singer and dancer during

Bada Singar), *Bahar Gauni* (performer outside the temple), *Gaudasini* (who fanned the deity with a flywhisk), *Patuari* (who performed before the procession idol) and *Maharis* were all housed in Mahari Pallavi or Anga Alsa Patna of Puri. They had prescribed rhythmic cycles - *Pahapata, Sarama, Parameswara, Malashree, Harachandi, Jhuti Atha Tali* - for the performance.

Intermittent attacks by rulers like Sultan Firoz Shah (1360), Hussain Shah Sultan of Bengal (1510) and Kalapahad, the General of Suleiman Karnani, disrupted temple ritual. With the decline of the Gangas, the degeneration of the *Mahari* began. By the mid-eighteenth century of Maratha rule, the temple dancer had come to be associated with concubinage.

Coinciding with the *Mahari* decline, rose the *Gotipua* tradition with pre-puberty boys trained to dance in female attire in keeping with the *Sakhi Nacha* tradition. The *Gotipua* danced outside the temple precincts during processions, *jatras* and festivals. These supple-bodied performers specialised in *Bandha Nriya*, an acrobatic form in which the dancer executes contortionist postures called *Chira, Nahunia, Mayura, Chara,* and *Sagadi* corresponding to some of the more gymnastic *Karanas* (dance units) mentioned in the *Natya Sastra* like *Mayuralalita, Gangavatarana,* and *Laltatilaka*. Though mentioned in texts like the *Sangeeta Darpana, Bandha Nritya* as a fully evolved tradition is a seventeenth-century development. Reduced to a degenerated form by the twentieth century, *Gotipua* still contained the basic vocabulary of movement and rhythm for Odissi in its new manifestation, for all the gurus were trained in it.

While Odissi embodies the *Mahari* and the *Gotipua* sensibilities, contemporary Odissi had its real beginnings in Orissa Theatres, with which each of the main Gurus Pankajcharan Das, Kelucharan Mohapatra, and Debaprasad Das were involved in the crucial forties.

A posthumous son of Kshetramani and Dharma Das who worked in the police, Guru Pankajcharan, imbibed his art from Fakira and his aunt Ratnaprabha, both *Maharis* with whom he grew up as a *Madali* player. Trained in *Gotipua*, he joined the Ranganath Dev Goswami and Bikhari Charan Dalei Ras Leela troupes before performing at the Hajuri Theatre of Puri. Later with New Theatres in Baripada, he was drawn to *Chhau*, the martial art form. Absorbed finally into Annapoorna Theatres, he came in contact with Kelucharan

Mohapatra, who also joined as a drummer.

A byword for Odissi today, Guru Kelucharan Mahapatra was born in a family of Patachitrakars. He followed his father's example, learning to play the *Khol*. A clandestine dance involvement began in an *akhada* under Balabhadra Sahu, a confectioner by caste. His considerable histrionic talent found an outlet when he joined the Ras Leela troupe of Mohansundar Dev Goswami. Leaving the troupe, and several odd assignments later, he found his way into Orissa Theatres founded in 1939 by Kalicharan Patnaik. Director Durlav Chandra Singh, recognising his talent, hired him on a monthly salary of seven rupees! The war years intervened till Kelucharan was recruited into Annapoorna B Theatre, comprising the breakaway actors from Orissa Theatres. A new art journey began for him, signalled by an eventful meeting with Pankajcharan Das hired as a dance teacher, with his old friend Durlav Chandra Singh and an enterprising manager Lingaraj Nanda who was willing to try out new ventures.

Deba Prasad Das, the other noteworthy Guru, was born in 1932 at Keul Chabi Sua village near Jhankada, famed for its Sarala temple, to a police inspector. He was barely one year old when his mother Indramani Devi expired. He was trained in traditional Oriya music comprising *Chhanda, Chaupadi, Keshaba Koili, Manobodha Chautisa,* and *Abakasha* items, by his paternal grandfather Bauribandhu Das, a violinist. Leaving studies, Deba Prasad joined the *Gotipua akhada* of the late Mohana Chandra Mohapatra. After dabbling in terracotta sculpting and painting, he ran away from home to join New Theatres where he specialised in female and comic roles. With Pankajcharan, Prasad trained in the *Mahari* approach.

Like all the others he soon found his way to Annapoorna Theatre's A and B groups, where he taught *Gotipua* dance to actors. Much later in life, he joined the National Music Association started in 1949, and then the Utkal Sangeet Natak Akademi set up in 1954, finally becoming a faculty member in the Utkal Sangeet Mahavidyalaya in 1964.

A momentous development for Odissi occurred when Pankajcharan Das choreographed the famous Mohini-Bhasmasura dance taking on the role of Bhasmasura himself with Kelucharan Mohapatra as Mahadev. For the role of Mohini, the theatre commissioned the services of a young actress,

Laxmipriya, who had been with Annapoorna A theatre almost from its inception. The simple ten-beat rhythm of Kelucharan Mohapatra's dance and the sixteen-beat dance of Mohini, created history with the Kelucharan-Laxmipriya duo becoming a popular pair. This culminated in Laxmipriya marrying Kelucharan Mohapatra. Lingraj Nanda, sensing the potential for luring theatre audiences through dance sequences, arranged for Lakmipriya to learn two items from *Gotipua* master Krishnachand Mahapatra based on the Oriya songs '*Nahin Ke Kari Dela*' and '*Jaano Re Mo Mana Parma Mita*'. Both became hits throughout Orissa, inspiring many a young girl into learning the dance, which at that time was clubbed under *Adhunika Geeta* having a mixed bag of items like Nataraj, Snake Charmer, Mayur, Hunter and so on. The other epoch-making item was *Dasavatar* composed in 1947 as a sequence in the play *Sadhavi Jhia* (The Merchant's Daughter). It was a combined effort with Durlav Chandra Singh contributing *Dhrupad Bols* which Kelucharan later changed to suit the Odissi vocabulary, and Pankajcharan working out the choreography with inputs from Kelucharan. The *Kalyan raga* score was by Durlav Chandra Singh and to this day, the item remains a more or less unchanged part of the Odissi repertoire.

The first stirrings of new dance in Orissa had been set in motion. Around that time Dayal Sharma, a student of Uday Shankar, visiting Orissa with his performing troupe, was impressed with Kelucharan Mohapatra and provided him some choreographic insight. Adding more muscle to the art scene was the Cuttack A.I.R. Station director, P. V. Krishnamurthy, who also helped with the score for dance drama productions choreographed by Kelucharan Mohapatra. By 1953, Krishnamurthy had joined the pioneering art institution, Kala Vikash Kendra, started by a Gujarati businessman Babulal Doshi.

Dance and music institutions began cropping up in the main towns of Cuttack and Bhubaneswar. The momentous event came in 1954 when Priyambada Mohanty danced, with Guru Debaprasad Das conducting the recital, for the Inter-University Festival at Delhi, the performance arousing unending curiosity in dance lovers. In 1957, supposedly provoked by Rukmini Devi's casual dismissal of Odissi as a still-evolving art, came the Jayantika effort with a group of gurus and scholars, Pankajcharan Das, Kelucharan Mohapatra, Debaprasad Das, Mayadhar Raut, and

scholars Raghunath Dutta, Dayanidhi Das and Dhirendra Patnaik taking a joint oath to collectively rebuild the dance. An entire vocabulary of movement and rhythmic syllables was built and rough edges were pruned. A whole new repertoire with a concert format of Mangalacharan, Batu Nritya, Pallavi, Abhinaya and Moksha was finalised by 1960. Providing the musical scaffolding were Balakrishna Das and Bhubaneswar Misra, along with others like Shyam Sunder Kar.

Meeting in the Raghunath temple in Telenga Bazar, Cuttack, or in the living room of Loknath Misra, a consensus was worked out on the invocatory item *Mangalacharan*, with the rhythmic syllables (*Bols*) composed by Balabhadra Sahu and Agadu Maharana, and dance by Kelucharan and Pankajcharan Das. The dance began with floral offerings to Lord Jagannath, the presiding deity of Orissa, and salutations to Bhumidevi in the manner of the *Mahari*. *Pallavi* as the visualisation of a musical composition of notes and rhythmic syllables set to a particular raga emerged as the mainstay of an Odissi recital. The original *Pallavis* by Balakrishna Das, like the *Basant Pallavi*, were patterned on tunes of traditional Odissi lyrics and succeeded by some of the most evocative compositions by Bhubaneswar Misra and others. The *abhinaya* part had a vast heritage of poetry by medieval poets like Kavisurya Baladev Rath, the 'most musical,' Gopal Krishna Patnaik, the 'most poetic', and Banamali, the 'most devotional'[9].

The item, *Batu*, became a bone of contention among the gurus, some interpreting it etymologically as coming from *vadu* meaning bondage with reference to the *Mahari*, and others connecting it to the Batuka Bhairava cult with the item created with statuesque postures reminiscent of temple sculpture. This was unacceptable to Pankajcharan Das and Debaprasad Das, each creating his own version of what is known as *Sthayi*. Each guru had his stylistic preferences reflected in the individual creations. With Guru Kelucharan Mohapatra inevitably becoming the first among equals, Jayantika, after the first flush of co-ordination, petered out. But Guru Kelucharan Mohapatra and Bhubaneswar Misra continued to form an excellent twosome, the musical compositions of one with the dance choreography of the other as if made for each other. Known for the lyricism of his style and ability for matching movement perfectly to the musical mood,

Kelucharan emphasises the non-use of the hip, all deflections of the upper body being dictated by the isolated torso or the *udvahita* movement. In the *abhinaya* department, able assistance came from Guru Mayadhar Raut, who after five years spent in Kalakshetra learning Bharatanatyam and Kathakali, proved to be of immense help in systematising, according to classical prescriptions, a vocabulary of hand gestures[10].

Among the many Odissi dancers making a mark, most are Guru Kelucharan's students, with the late Sanjukta Panigrahi being the foremost. Along with singer husband, Raghunath Panigrahi, this passionate dancer symbolises the best in Odissi.

Pankajcharan, 'the Guru of Gurus', is famous for the delicacy of interpretative dance. Some of his *atibhangi* or extreme bodily deflections, unique gait and use of space and transitions in group choreography which veers away from the frontal aspected dance, have influenced all dancers, though he cannot claim anyone among the established dancers as being solely his student. His famous production, *Pancha Kanya*, reveals a very liberated approach to woman, an attitude imbibed from the *Mahari* association. Ratna Roy, now settled in the United States, is the only dancer to have trained exclusively under this guru.

Debaprasad Das spent precious years roaming the world with Indrani Rehman, his prime pupil, who was undoubtedly largely instrumental in putting Odissi on the international map. Away from the main Odissi scene at home, Guru Debaprasad returned to find that history had passed him by. By the time he joined the Utkal Sangeet Mahavidyalaya in 1965 as a teacher, it was too late. A conservative guru, who disapproved of speed in a style given to acute body deflections, Debaprasad also had an informed liberal side, accepting inspiration from the tribal and non-classical streams of Orissan art. His style emphasised minimalism, with no embroidery of elaborations built round the musical line. The earthy vigour of his *sabda, swara, patha* approach with words often recited in their poetic metre, instead of being strung to melody, is suitable for the male dancer. Ramli Ibrahim, a Malaysian, ranks among the best male dancers of Odissi. Debaprasad's Odissi has a strong *Gotipua* flavour and some of his early students like Vijayalakshmi Mohanty started off as excellent Bandha Nritya dancers. His dance drama, *Manini*, was the earliest in this genre

76

Heroic postures adopted by
Malaysian dancer Ramli
Ibrahim.
Facing page: Dancer Reela
Hota depicts the secret look,
synchronising mood and
movement.
Preceding page 74: Sonal
Mansingh as Krishna with the
flute and as a gracefully
seated *nayika* with hands
linked in the *potala mudra*.
Preceding page 75:
Madhavi Mudgal smells
a flower.

of work, created for the National Music Association. Today, his principle student Durga Charan Ranbir has several good students to his credit.

The highly individualistic Odissi style of Guru Surendranath Jena, influenced by the Tantra and temple sculpture, is not widely prevalent, its best exponent being the Guru's daughter Pratibha Jena.

Stylistically Odissi revolves round the *Tribhanga* as the central posture. The head, torso and lower half of the body in deflections, with each part bent in opposition to the part above, creates the three-bend figure, which along with the square half-seated *Chauka* that has the feet kept apart and the knees flexed sideways, forms the core stylistic posture. The sideways movement of the isolated torso is a very special feature[11]. Very lyrical when the dancer has the fluidity enabling the constant change of levels demanded in Odissi, the dance could look very jerky if rendered by unfinished performers. Pirouettes or *brahmaris* executed clockwise and counter-clockwise with the dancer maintaining the level of the half-seated position are another important feature. The graceful zigzag walk both forwards and backwards with one foot anchored while the other does an arch in the air to end with the dancer in a crossed feet posture is very typical.

The music for Odissi has evoked flak from certain quarters for losing its regional identity by being influenced by the Hindustani and the Carnatic systems. It was music which first earned the 'Odissi' appellation because of its specific identity, the dance acquiring it later. The late Jivan Pani, a musicologist and scholar, cited examples from treatises like *Gita Prakash* written by Krishnadas Badajena Mohapatra, a famous poet/musician in the court of Akbar, mentioned in Abul Fazal's work, in support of his argument of Odissi music having a definite classical identity, different from both the Hindustani and the Carnatic[12]. As a bridge between the south and the north, the cultural influences of both regions have blended in Orissa, though its regional lyrics like the *Champu* and *Janana* and the cadence and metre of its vast poetic heritage have a very distinct quality. Perhaps due to waning patronage amidst political turmoil, the legacy of structured lyrics was handed down the generations while the improvisatory abstract part, like *raga alap* and weaving of off-the-cuff solfa passages, got stunted. When a new dance edifice was being conceived, there was no corpus of abstract musical

compositions (like the *Jatiswaram* or the *Tillana* in Bharatanatyam) readily available for the non-thematic part of the dance, which had to form the core substance. The interpretative part, with the plethora of poetic compositions, faced no such problem. Of the two notable composers but for whom Odissi would not have acquired a new repertoire of scores, Bhubaneswar Misra was trained in Carnatic music (apart from knowing Hindustani music too) under Dwaram Venkataswamy Naidu, the great violinist, while Balakrishna Das had studied under Bade Ghulam Ali Khan. The two musical influences thus became inevitable. Even now in the state-run Utkal Sangeet Mahavidyalaya, where the Hindustani system and the traditional Oriya music are being taught to students, there is no consensus on how 'typical Odissi *ragas*' are to be developed. Delving into old texts to revive *ragas* cannot establish a tradition, which evolves from several creative musicians singing a *raga*, to give it an identifiable architectonic authenticity. Dancer Sonal Mansingh with guidance from Jivan Pani and the services of a singer like Bankim Sethi has worked at reconstructing *ragas* mentioned in the *Gita Govind*, guided by the old textual prescriptions. But unless backed by a similar endeavour by many others such attempts will remain individual efforts, not become part of a movement.

Though late to enter the dance arena, Odissi has acquired a large following in all major Indian cities and even abroad to the extent of an Odissi Seminar being held in Canada in 2000. The effects of such proliferation are inevitably being felt in the varying proficiency levels and a disappearing *Chauka*. Shrill criticism about 'more of the same thing' has created a wariness even amongst Gurus who are baffled by this refrain after having created a whole new dance edifice. The same story as other dances, Odissi also has too many aspirants with not too many performance opportunities. The high degree of theatricality in contemporary expressional dance is palpable to senior dancers like Minati Das who belong to a time when *abhinaya* was less ornamented and simpler. She feels that the individual Gurus have evolved in very distinctive ways over the years, for when she was trained, stylistic differences were not pronounced. Odissi is largely the female dancer's domain, the male dancer all too often relegated to teaching. More male dancers have emerged from the Debaprasad school.

The dance drama genre has become a popular way

Kavita Dwibedi is shown progressing through the stages of an Odissi dance item in a movement montage.

of communicating with audiences not familiar with the stylised language. The dancer most willing to experiment and explore is Sonal Mansingh who has created an entire repertoire of her own compositions With research and ideological thrust provided by the late Jivan Pani, she has drawn from Orissa's narrative traditions like the *Pala*, from folk tales and from Buddhist *Charia* poetry. Dancers like Madhavi Mudgal, who has produced works like *Sohamasmi*, *Ganga* to *Mekong* and many *Pallavi* compositions designed for a group, and Sharmila Biswas of Kolkata, who has conceived of productions like *Shoorpanakha* and one on the life of the *Mahari*, have done notable work. The dance establishment in Orissa, the home of the dance, is less enthusiastic about innovative work deeming it distorting tradition – a rigidity no doubt prompted by the need to preserve what has been rebuilt with much effort. Gurus like Kelucharan have used the martial vigour of *Chhau* blended with the lyrical grace of Odissi *bhangis* in works like *Eklavya*.

Not much known amongst Odissi circles, Ratna Roy, who heads the dance faculty of the Evergreen State College in Olympia, Washington, has used the medium of Odissi for themes on women's liberation. 'Doongri Mahari always said to my guru that there is no more liberated person than the *Mahari*, who was answerable to no man,' she says.

In Orissa, do-gooders, earnestly guarding tradition which in the present form is not more than half a century old, have repudiated all new work as being disloyal to the gurus in that it goes beyond the prescribed boundaries they set. Even when original work has been inspired by narrative traditions within Orissa like *Pala*, *Daskatia* or *Prahlad Nataka*, it has rarely found acceptance. This rigidity is doubtless prompted by fears of losing every thing that hard work and application have erected. It is often forgotten that even a guru like Kelucharan Mohapatra has used *Chhau* movements in *Eklavya*. The martial vigour of the *Chhau* movements has blended with the lyrical grace of Odissi *bhangis* in a fine canvas of contrasts. Even Jivan Pani, had he lived in Orissa, would have found less urge for experimenting.

Guru Kelucharan Mohapatra philosophically sums up: 'We gurus have done our bit to ensure the survival of the dance. Now it is up to the next generation to carry it forward.' Knowing what has been accomplished in the span of half a century, one can hardly grumble about Odissi not changing with the times.

Kathakali

On a bare stage without props, symbolising the expanse of space or *akash*, to the *sabda* or sound of the assertive drums and slow-spun music, the actor in weird get-up evokes through his art a larger-than-life experience. The burning flame from the wicks of the giant oil lamp in front casts a strange glow on the green and black painted faces, the reddened eyes moving with phenomenal expressiveness. This is Kathakali, largely confined to its regional Kerala environs, and the least understood of the classical performing art traditions of India.

Kathakali revels in the confrontation of opposites, its heroes and anti-heroes from the *Puranas* and epics acting out their desires and antagonisms in unabashedly exaggerated theatre: a demon in the comely disguise of Lalita transforming into a hideous, writhing Pootana in the throes of death, her life breath drained out by baby Krishna sucking at her poison-tipped breasts. Or Bhima abandoning his princely bearing and transforming to a bloodthirsty fiend clawing out the entrails of Dussasana. Kathakali presents a world of Olympian proportions, 'bizarre, subhuman and superhuman at once,' to quote C. J. Jung. Beneath all the seemingly unbridled emotion, lies an art technique of immense skill and subtlety.

Paradoxically, the painted faces hiding the real person under the thick coat of colour, are designed to highlight each facial muscle moving in a grand play of emotion. Rendered in the open temple courtyard, its performance ritual notwithstanding, Kathakali has little connection with temple ritual in the sanctum. Even while dealing with themes from mythology, the dance has a strongly secular character, its godly heroes and demoniac villains lying outside the realm of worship and devotion. Significantly, the Kathakali Krishna is not the delightful prankster going after dairy delights nor a romancing hero. He is here the crafty war strategist.

In a matrilineal society, Kathakali evolved as an all-male tradition, the female roles played by male artistes being small but thematically central. Down the years, performers specialising in *stree vesha* have gained distinction. Once drawn into the intricate theatrical web of the dance, it is well nigh impossible to lay off the Kathakali bug and not become a *Kathakali Brantha*, the nickname for the Kathakali addict.

Kathakali evolved as a blend of artistic influences from Kerala's multiple performing art forms, starting

from the ancient *Chakyar Koottu*, a surviving remnant of Sanskrit theatre, '*attams*' like Kaliyattam, Kutiyattam, Krishnattam, Ramanattam and a plethora of other traditions like Teyyam, Mudiyettu, and various *tullals*[1].

Mid-seventeenth century Kerala comprised several major and minor kingdoms. Prince Kottarakkara Thampuran wrote a musical dance drama in eight parts, setting in motion the Ramanattam tradition as a counterpoint to the already existing Krishnanattom of King Manavendra, the provocation being the refusal by the Zamorin of Calicut (Kozhikkode) to send the Krishnanattom troupe to Travancore. With a libretto blending Malayalam and Sanskrit[2], Ramanattam became a role model for Kathakali plays with the art form spreading to Vettom in central Kerala. In time, new aspects like the *pacha* or green make-up for the heroic characters, the *Chenda* percussion, and the specially designed large pleated skirts worn over the trousers came into vogue. Kottayam Thampuran (1675-1725) of north Kerala re-composed the dance form, introducing heroic characters like the Pandava princes, injecting a potent histrionic element into the play. The make-up was systematised with a white border (*Chutti*) outlining the face to accentuate expressions. The presentation became more elaborate. Little is know of individual performers of the time, barring two names, Vellattu Chattunni Panicker and his disciple Naanu Menon.

Mid-eighteenth-nineteenth century Kathakali had the patronage of Kartika Tirunal Maharaja of Travancore and Veera Kerala Varma of Cochin. Kaplingadam Namboodiri, a reformer, introduced new facets with anti-heroes emerging as powerful counter-pointing characters. The early nineteenth century was a low point till the art acquired an ardent patron in Utram Tirunal of the Travancore royal family. Different Kathakali styles came up, like the *Kalluvazhi* style under Ollappamanna Mana, noted for technical virtuosity. Under Unniri Panikar, the *Kalladikkodan* and *Kaplingadan* styles merged and Pattikkamtodi Ramunni Menon later patented this style in Kerala Kalamandalam. The *Takazhi* and *Karipuzha* styles, influenced by Kutiyattam were more interpretative. A far more leisurely pace giving room for textual elaboration became the vogue with palace troupes or *Kaliyogams* becoming well known. Artistes like Kandiyon Pappu Pillai, Takazhi Velu Pillai, and Kochayyappa Panikar became stars. The mid-nineteenth century to 1930 was another lean period with troupes

disbanded due to diminishing royal patronage. Strangely enough, the 1860-1900 period saw enhanced literary activity with many new *attakathas* (literary texts for Kathakali) being written. Of all the Kaliyogam artistes, Pattikkantodi Ramunni Menon alone devoted himself to training students, many of whom became Kathakali giants like Kalamandalam Krishnan Nair, Keezhpadam Kumaran Nair, Kalamandalam Ramankutty Nair, Padmanabhan Nair.

Just when Kathakali seemed on its last legs, Vallathol Narayana Menon, a prominent Malayalam poet and editor of *Keralodayam*[3], and Mukunda Raja took charge. Gathering scattered expertise under one agency, they started the Kerala Kalamandalam in 1930. The institution was housed in 1937 at Cherutturutti on the banks of the Nila river, and referred to as 'Bharata Puzha'. Stars like Pattikkantodi Ramunni Menon, Kunju Kurup, Kavalappara Narayanan Nair, singers Samikutty Bhagavatar and Venkatakrishna Bhagavatar, *Chenda* giant Moottamana Namboodiri, *Maddlam* player Venkicchan and Madhava Warrier came together – not on the *Gurukulam* pattern but for pooling the talent of the *Vadakkan* (northern) *Chitta* and *Thekkan* (southern) *Chitta* styles. Ramunni Menon favoured the Kalluvazhi style, which Kalamandalam actors mainly followed.

Institutions sprang up in Kerala: the Unaayi Varrier Kalanilayam at Irinjalakuda, P.S.V. Natyasangham at Kottakkal, G.S.S. Kathakali Academy at Perur and the Gandhi Seva Sangh Kathakali Academy at Palakkad founded by Sadanam Kumaran Nair in 1954. Inspired by a Kathakali enthusiast, the late Appukuttan Nair, Margi came up in 1969 as a resource centre for grooming excellence with fresh poetic inputs and varied intellectual and expert guidance. Vallathol, who even travelled to Santiniketan with a Kathakali troupe, passed away in 1958. Much before in 1941, Kalamandalam, faced with scarce financial resources, had been handed over to the state government. Dogged by administrative problems, the institution today is still considered the premier centre for Kathakali training.

Every aspect of the art – its strong body language, the enormous weight of the skirt and headgear worn by the actors, the voice, breath control and unerring timing called for in the slow-paced singing and the percussion by standing drummers with the heavy instruments slung from the shoulder and fastened at the waist – makes severe physical and mental demands. There is a high

degree of physical discipline with a gruelling eight to ten hours of daily practice and rigorous oil massage during the monsoon months to make the body supple. This was accepted by students recruited mostly from the Nair militia and from subordinates of patron families. With exercises (*mei sadhakam*) like vertical jumps (*karanam mariyuka*), high jumps (*Chattam*), the needle-sitting position in a complete split (*suchikirikkuka*), footwork in four tempi (*kaal sadakham*), eye exercises (*kannu sadhakam*) with clarified butter applied to make eyeballs supple, the training that begins at 2.30 a.m. is not for the faint hearted.

The *marumakkatayam* institution[4] was more matrilineal in Kerala than matriarchal. But women managed to make inroads into the male preserves of Kathakali. *Kathakali Rangam* by K.P.S. Menon mentions one Kathyayani (eighteenth century) famed for the *chuvanna tadi* (red-bearded) Sugreeva role with the greatest actor as Bali, nicknamed Bali Othickon, partnering her. One Vanchiyoor Kathyayani Amma (born circa 1880), daughter of a reputed Kathakali actor Kuchu Nilakantha Pillai, was famed for playing Krishna in Kuchelavrittam and Rajasooyam. Among students of Ramunni Menon, was a woman from Vellinezhi or Palakkad called Munnoorkod Kaippencheri Kunhimala Amma. Ragini Devi, mother of late dancer Indrani, who even underwent the *Uzhichil* (oil massage) and Shanta Rao and more recently the late Kalyanikuttyamma, Satyabhama, Kanak Rele – all Mohini Attam exponents – have been Kathakali trained. An all-female troupe of married women working in other professions, with even singing and percussion by female artistes, Tripunithura Vanitha Sangam, in 1991 even performed at the Mecca of Kathakali, Kerala Kalamandalam. Roles like Duryodhana and Dussasana were played – the only give away being the gold bangles round Duryodhana's wrists!

Kalamandalam, which does not accept long-term female students, does enrol foreign women for short stints. Gender equations are determined by the socio-historical context. The argument that the massage is gynaecologically harmful to women and also that the naturally supple woman's body does not need *uzhichil* may well be convenient explanations built round the all-male approach. The International Centre for Kathakali at Delhi is training several women students. But the energy of the dance is suited to the male physique.

Kathakali's non-human world of the imagination,

Mukhabhinaya, literally 'face-acting', by the late Krishnan Nair, the Kathakali doyen.

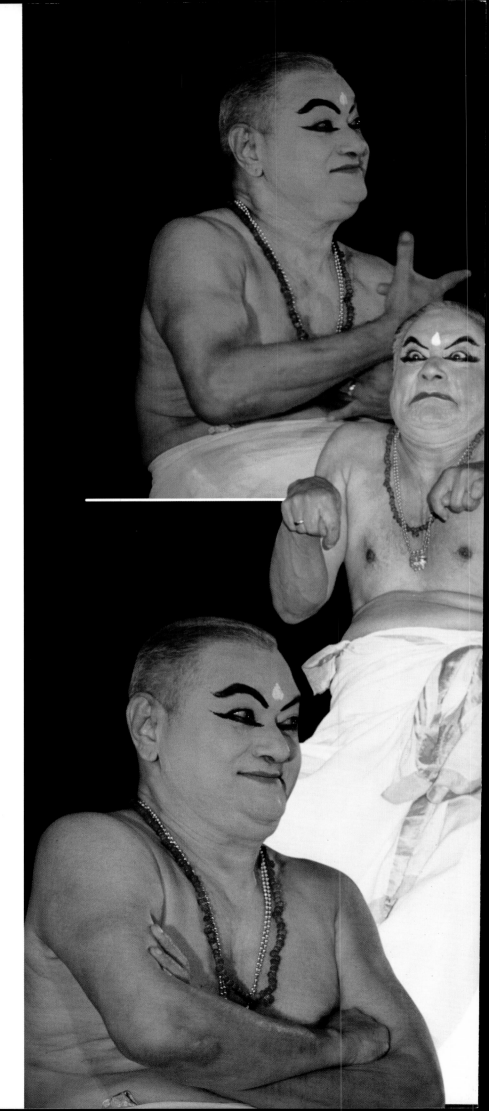

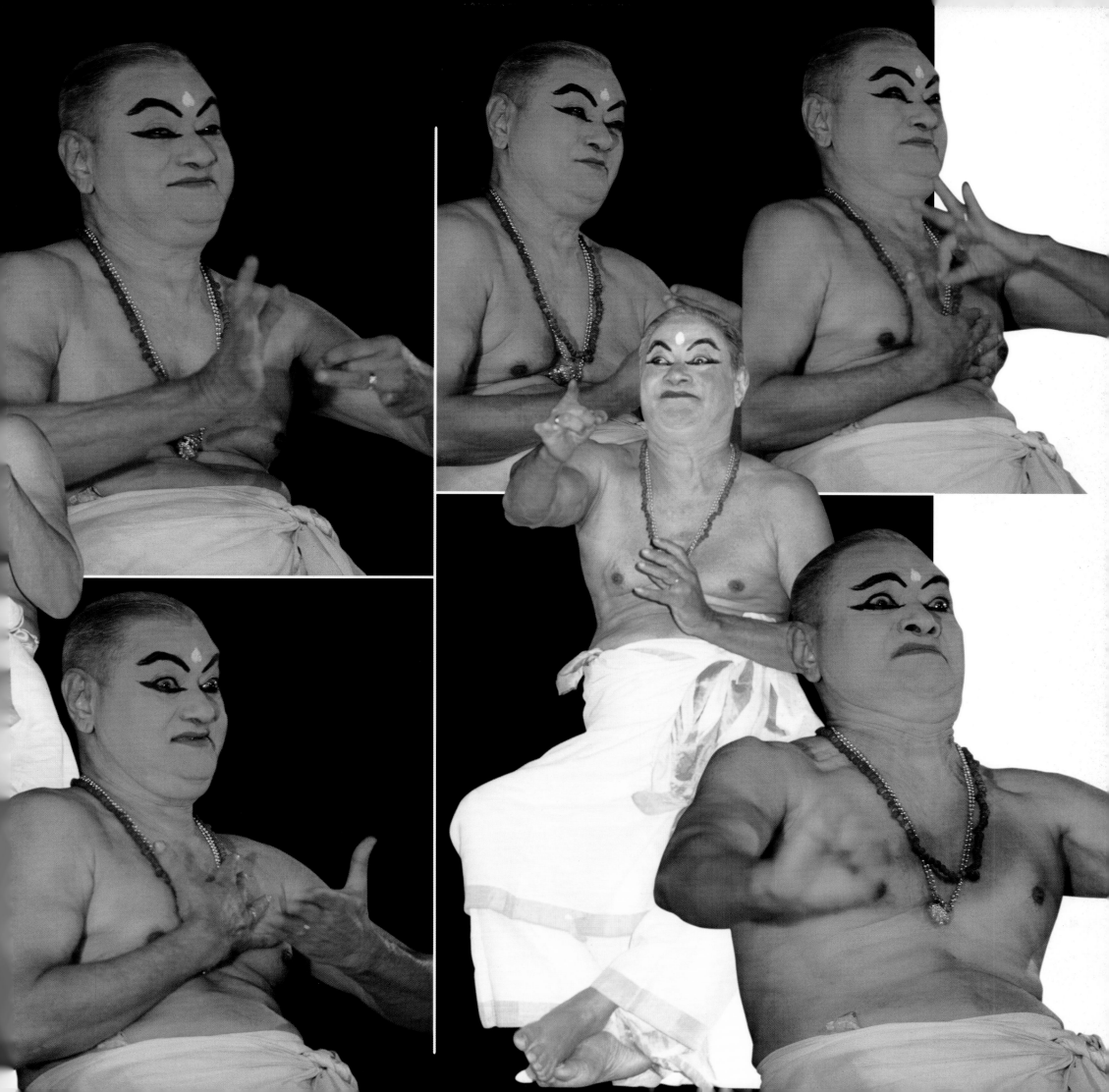

Chennittala Chellappan Pillai as Krishna and Govindan Kutty in *stree vesham* (woman's form) as Draupadi in the play *Duryodhanavadham*.

distanced from the mundane behaviour of the everyday world, except for realistically treated characters like a carpenter or Brahmin, has its unique grandeur and majesty. Amidst heightening suspense, its epic characters reveal themselves in stages to the audience from behind a cloth curtain held by two persons (*tirasila*). Manipulating the curtain via a special dramatic device with only face and hands revealing character is called *tiranokku*. *Abhinaya* in Kathakali takes on a new dimension with every isolated facial muscle involved in elaborate expressional language.

Highly stylised, the make-up emphasises character types. Heroic roles like those of Arjuna and Nala have green make-up (*pacha*) with elongated eyes. The aggressive *Katti* characters have a basic green foundation, broken up by a red painted moustache with white pith stuck on the nose giving it a bulbous look. Some of the strongest Kathakali roles like Duryodhana, Keechaka, and Ravana are from this category. The destructive red bearded (*chuvanna tadi*) characters are with the *chutti* made up of square, paper cut-outs sticking out from either side of the nose, black smudged eyes adding a fearsome look. Uncommon characters like those of Kirata, the hunter, or an aborigine belong to the black-bearded (*Karutta Tadi*) group, the black beard and basic black of the face touched by red and white. Half human and half animal characters like Hanuman, Nandikeswara, and Dwividha are in the white-bearded (*Veluppu Tadi*) category. Demons from the *Kari* group have a black face with elaborate red moustaches. Women, Brahmins, fighters and saints are in the *minukku* slot with plain, flesh-coloured make-up. Within these types, the changes in minutae are in accordance with the characterisation.

The actor evokes a stylised world with his elaborate vocabulary of hand gestures, set to subtle micro rhythms. The prescribed rhythmic interludes or *Kalasam* incorporating jumps, sideway shifts of movement and leaps, while not indicative of emotion, support both mood and character. An aggressive character would perform the *Valiakalasam*. A slower *Kalasam* with gentler foot contact would go with a love sequence. *Kalasam* can also be used to evoke humour. The angry character is more apt to hammer the floor with the turned-in edges of the feet, forming wide arcs while placing one foot as far away from the other as possible.

In the Kathakali narrative, a character takes on

different roles, even when the *aharya* (get-up) reinforces an established identity. Through his perspective, the audience gets to visualise another character, like the smitten Keechaka composing a song and dance poem of Sailandhri's gait and beauty. As pointers to the character's state of mind, these passages offer scope for the actor's creative ability. Nala's description of Damayanti in Nalacharitam is a case in point[5]. One Bhima's forest wanderings in *Kalyanasowgandhikam* in search of an exotic flower for wife Draupadi can, through the dance narrative, evoke a feel of the entire forest and jungle law[6].

The accompanying *Sopanam* style of singing[7] is believed to have acquired Carnatic shadings under Kavaseri Bhagavatar. Today, *Sopanam* employs *ragas* identifiable in the Carnatic idiom as well as melodic modes indigenous to it like *Indalam, Padi, Kanakurinji,* and *Navarasa*. Music in Kathakali is for enhancing the drama and not for virtuosity with *raga alapana* and *swaraprasthara* improvisation. But, clarity of enunciation and sustaining hours of slow-paced singing demand not just musical acumen but also strong vocal cords. Which is the reason for distributing the burden between two singers, the principal vocalist (*Ponnani*) setting the pace, while providing the *tala* on the *Chengila* (gong), and the second (*singidi*) taking on from where he leaves while playing on the *ilattalam* (cymbals). An *adanta tala* of 56 *matras* well sung, with an actor of the level of Kalamandalam Gopi as Nala interpreting the musical line, evokes the sensibilities of love, with a subtext flowing out of the actor's imagination.

The assertive *Chenda* drum, slung vertically and played on top with sticks, forms the lifeline of the performance. The *Maddalam* is strapped horizontally to the waist of the percussionist and played on both sides with strapped fingers; the small *edekka* is rubbed with a stick to produce a range of musical sounds. Renowned Krishnankutty Poduval's *Chenda* playing for demon or saint would even catch the feel of flowers strewn on the floor, as mimed by actor Ramunni Menon. The same *Chenda* expert, challenged by Raman Kutty Nair to accompany his *illakkiyattam* (improvisations accompanied by percussion), was not found wanting.

Kathakali's central half-seated position with out-turned knees has the two feet spaced apart to form a square. The floor stomping is with the outer soles of inward facing feet. Covering space in squares and

triangles, movements include full leg extensions and jumps. Dancing in restricted space, with singers at the back and percussionists on the right, the actor creates a feel of largeness and expanse. By climbing a one-foot tall stool, he can become a heavenly being.

Pattikkamtodi Ramunni Menon trained under the Kodungaloor royal family with gurus Kochunni Thampuran and Kunjunni Thampuran. He learnt *swarvayu*, an intricate science of breathing according to the musical notes, the variations in muscle tension and air pressure adding depth to emotion and acting. There is an oft-narrated incident: while playing the role of Keechaka, Ramunni Menon's stillness on stage fooled even his wife into taking him for dead. Guru Sadanam Balakrishnan [8] of the International Centre for Kathakali, Delhi, complains actors today have no inkling of this science, nor do they have the patience to understand it.

An ensemble form, Kathakali in technique cannot be changed by individual dancers. Confronted by dwindling audiences, lessening performance platforms and a precarious economic future, Kathakali faces a challenge today. The daunting training routine can be undertaken by very few and even Kalamandalam, with dwindling recruits each year, has problems in attracting new talent and quality teachers. Lecture demonstrations seem to pay more than actual performances. 'This is an art for the connoisseur. When a four-hour play has to be condensed to less than half its duration to suit uninitiated audiences, what happens to an art whose soul is elaboration?" questions Guru Sadanam Balakrishnan. 'Kathakali jewellery, so vital, is today made by only one family. *Vadakkan Chitta* is already lost. To sustain at least what one has, the art form needs strong government support. We will otherwise lose it,' is the guru's observation. With Kalamandalam Krishnan Nair no more, with Ramankutty Nair much beyond seventy and Kalamandalam Gopi nearing seventy, Kathakali sees no giants-in-the-making. What is disquieting is that even in the temple court yard performances in Kerala, where Kathakali used to reign supreme, the art form now has to share space along with several other performing traditions and cut short its programmes.

Contrary to popular perception, Kathakali has a rare ability to absorb outside influences and respond to changes. Unlike other rehearsed dances, each Kathakali performance is a synergy of scattered actors assembled just for the performance. Ever dynamic, even as early as 1916, a performance of *Narakasura vadham* was presented on the makeshift stage of a Syrian Christian's private garden for a three hundred-strong Tiya and Nair audience, according to the English monograph of A. Meerwarth. The monograph was based on a description by Frenchman M.A.Guerinot – a summary of which appears in the late Mohan Khokar's *SRUTI* article, 'Taking in Kathakali Thousand Moons ago'.

The only form already deconstructed into micro units for its training process, the potential of Kathakali has been recognised by specialised theatre groups in the country and abroad. Right from the twenties and thirties, persons like Uday Shankar and later Rukmini Devi found training in this medium the ideal preparation for male dancers, it is particularly good. The ability to isolate each facial muscle makes Kathakali excellent training for theatre aspirants. 'The challenge lies in your musculature speaking through all that paint. One is simultaneously playing with rhythm, with *mudra*, with emotion, with footwork, with powerful theatre, with text, with music – it is extraordinary,' says Maya Rao[9], whose work *Khol Do* based on Hassan Manto's short story is a contemporary creation, drawing on her Kathakali energy.

Vallathol himself tried themes like 'Killing of Hitler' and 'Gandhi's Victory' in Kathakali, though not very successfully. In 1987, Iyyamgode Sridharan's *Manavijayam* (People's Victory) propagated communist ideology, again without much success. The Kalamandalam production of *King Lear*, and Sadanam Balakrishnan's of *Othello* for the International Centre for Kathakali have played to world audiences.

Since 1930 when Alice Boner was mesmerised with the art form, her writings managed to convert people like Ebwerhard Fischer, director Folkteaterm Gavleborg. World Theatre personalities like Grotosky and Eugenie Barba have been drawn to Kathakali. Australian ballet dancer Louise Lightfoot, after her sojourn at Cherutturutti with Kalamandalam, started a Kathakali journey in her own country, where today Tara Rajkumar (at Melbourne) still runs a school for training students in the art form. According to Maya Rao, the Kathakali energy will always find other outlets. 'The *Chenda* player if denied a platform through Kathakali will go to *Pancha Vidyam*, where it will always have a place. In some form, the training will be expressed.' True, but only if the training in its traditional rigour exists. And for that the classical form has to be sustained as the mother source.

Mohini Attam

ohini Attam, literally Dance of the Enchantress, has its seeds in the deep past of Kerala. Its present form, designed exclusively for the female dancer, is, however, a recent creation inspired by the living matrix of Kerala's social ensemble dances performed on festive occasions like *Kaikottikali* and *Thiruvathirakali* [1], and *Nangyar Kootu*, the female component of the highly stylised Kutiyattam, a survivor of Sanskrit theatre. The repertoire of Mohini Attam, which had no temple connections or a Kootambalam history, has nevertheless a strong devotional element. Kerala scholars maintain the region has no history of *devadasi*-like women, and any evidence to the contrary is a spillover from Tamil areas with which Kerala history was interwoven[2].

The writer of the first Tamil epic, *Silappadikaram*, was King Ilango who belonged to the Chera dynasty, which ruled over Kadalmalainadu, comprising the Malabar area of Kerala. The earliest reference to the Cheras in the Ashokan rock edict II (circa 250 b.c.) describes the king as *Keralaputta* (*Keralaputra*), meaning son of Kerala. The Pallavas of Kanchipuram are known to have been great patrons of the Chakyars whose tradition of Kutiyattam is still prevalent.

Manipravala Kavyas are full of references to the female dancer called Unni, Unniyadi, Unnicheruthevi, Cherukara Kuttathi, and Uniachi. *Ganikas* attached to certain temples were considered to be women of low repute. But women dancers were attached to Suchindram and Tripunithura temples, one dancing to Tamil lyrics and the other doing a dance identifiable as neither Mohini Attam nor Bharatanatyam. Surely such instances could hardly have existed in a vacuum.

Historical evidence proves the existence of *Tali Nangyar* (*Tali* meaning temple, and *Nangyar* meaning woman) doing solo dance. The 932 A.D. Chollur and the 934 A.D. Nedumpara Tali inscriptions respectively mention one Chittarayil Nangyar donating land to the temple, and payments being made to Nangyar and Nattuvanar. A performance at Trikkanamatikalam temple is described in the thirteenth-century *Manipravala Champu Sukhasandesam*[3]. The *Tali Nangyars* are interpreted as belonging to three categories: *Uttama* or exalted women, generally from the aristocracy and pledged to celibacy; *Madhyama*, assisting the *tantris* in their *kriyas*; and *dasis* who were meant for menial tasks in the temple. The purely devotional dance,

Avayavam, rendered to a short verse, *Pann*, or to a chant with just a bell providing rhythm had little footwork, being performed seated. The *Tali Nangyars*, according to historians, were never bound to the deity like the *devadasis*[4]. Whatever be the relationship, by the fourteenth century, little remained of the conservative, isolated *Tali Nangya*. By the sixteenth-seventeenth centuries, theatrical forms favouring the male dancer, like Krishnattam, Ramanattom and later Kathakali, put the solo female dance into the shade. Some believe no one was allowed to witness the *Tali Nangaiy*'s dance. Only *Nangyar Kootu* survived as a female tradition since Kutiyattam received temple patronage.

The word, *Mohini*, occurs in an eighteenth-century Malayalam commentary of the *Vyavaharamala* composed two hundred years earlier by Mazhamangalam Narayanan Nambudiri. Much later the creator of Ottam Thullal, Kunjan Nambiar in his Goshayatra mentions Mohini Attam. Words like *Mohininilaye* and *Mohinisthana* occur in Maharaja Kartik Tirunal Balarama Verma's (1724–1798 A.D.) *Balaramabharata*, one of the most significant post-sixteenth century treatises on the performing arts of Kerala. But none of this gives an inkling of the dance prevailing at the time[5].

In Kerala, the Sanskritic culture of the Namboodiris and the martial tradition of the Nairs were assimilated into the art forms, thanks to the social custom of Namboodiri alliances with Nair women. In fact, Thampurans, born out of the wedlock of *Kshatriya* princes with Namboodiri women, became individual rulers of principalities.

By the thirteenth century, the three important royal houses were those of the Zamorin of Calicut, the Raja of Cochin and of Travancore. It was the last of these royal groups that traced succession through the female line. A regent in the late seventeenth century was Asvati Tirunal Umayamma Rani. His grandson, Marthanda Verma, a great Vishnu devotee, declared that he and his successors would govern as the subjects of Lord Vishnu seen as Padmanabha, the rightful ruler of the land. A staunch Vaishnavite faith has ever since been a feature of this area. Also worshipped here is the powerful female divinity, *Bhagavati*, the cult having strong Tantric overtones. Keralites are also worshippers of *Hariharaputra Ayyappa*, conceived of the Siva and Vishnu-as-Mohini union. Indeed, the *nayika* in Mohini Attam is always portrayed pining for Lord Padmanabha[6].

Representing the forces of both sustenance and cohesion, Vishnu – embodying reposeful energy as he reclines on his coiled-serpent couch, afloat on a vast milky ocean – took the form of enchantress Mohini at crucial moments in myth, when the gods proved helpless in the battle for righteousness. As the gods and demons churned the ocean, Mohini cast a spell of enchantment on the demons and succeeded in distributing the pot of elixir among the gods only. Mohini also came to the rescue of Siva, who was being pursued by the demon Bhasmasura, the recepient of a boon from Siva himself. The boon empowered the demon to reduce to ashes anybody on whom he placed his hand. Bhasmasura wanted to use the boon against Siva! Mohini lured Bhasmasura away with the promise that he would possess her if he won a dance competition against her. Mohini induced the demon, imitating every movement of hers, into placing his hand on his own head[7].

The murals of Padmanabhapuram and Mattancheri palaces testify to the Mohini myth's popularity. Mohini Attam stands for enchantment rather than seduction and, experts say, the stress is on dance as transformation – embodied in the act of the male god becoming a female[8]. Mohini Attam can mean both dance as enchantment and the dancer as enchantress.

Reformer Vallathol traced the dance right down to the days of the *Silappadikaram* because of the definite reference to Kerala's *Chakyars* while scholars like Pisharoti believed the dance had a six hundred-year-old history. Dancer Kanak Rele holds that aspects of female dance discussed in *Balaramabharatam* must be taken as referring to Mohini Attam since the codification of *hastas* here is different from that found in the other main treatise, *Hastalakshanadipika*, to which Kathakali relates. The influences of Dasiattam cannot be ruled out. Ullur Parameswara Iyer mentions in his Malayalam commentary that Maharaja Swati Tirunal, taken up with Dasiattam, instructed courtier Karutedatta Chomatiri to promote this dance under the name of Mohini Attam[9]. Two Tanjore quartet brothers, Vadivelu and Sivanandam, after the fall of the Maratha kingdom in Tanjore, moved over to the court of Maharaja Tirunal as did two dancers from Tanjore, Nirajakshi and Satyabhama. The Maharaja is also said to have married a dancer, Sugandhavalli.

Tirunal, himself a lyricist and composer, provided compositions for the female dance tradition. Gracing his court was a Tanjore musician, Parameswara

Dancer Deepti Omcheri
Bhalla is as serene as a lotus
in bloom.

Bhagavatar. Hardly surprising then that excepting for *Cholkettu* – which resembled the *Sabdam* in Dasiattam with the accent on verses invoking Bhagavati or Vishnu, and an interwoven element of *nritta* or rhythmic non-interpretative dance – performed in place of the *Alaripu*, the format followed was similar to Bharatanatyam with *Jatiswaram*, *Varnam*, *Padam*, and *Tillana*. The music was Carnatic. With Tirunal's death, a depleted treasury and British suzerainty sent whatever remained of solo female dance scurrying to Central Kerala for support.

It is clear that when Vallattol and Mukunda Raja began reviving the Kerala dances, solo female dance did not meet their standards of stylisation and dignity. Existing items like the *Mukkutti* dance with the song 'Endamukkutti kandathundo?' (Have you seen my nose ring?), and the *Kalabham koothu*, both rather pedestrian in treatment, seemed apt for titillation. In the first, the dancer moved from man to man in what was deemed inappropriate intimacy, looking for the nose ring. Despite the provocative gestures, some witnesses testify to the movement as well as the *abhinaya* of the performers not being devoid of artistic merit. In the other item *Kalabham koothu*, the dancer as the *nayika* preparing herself for a meeting with the lover, extolled the cooling effect of sandal paste on the body, helping to calm the fever of unrequited love[10]. With the advent of the British, British resident Colonel Monroe imposed an official ban on Mohini Attam in the states of Travancore and Cochin.

Even during the last half century, great Carnatic vocalists like the late G. N. Balasubramaniam and Semmangudi Srinivasa Iyer provided the score for innumerable Swati Tirunal compositions, differing from the original scores later discovered.

The indigenous *Sopanam* music resembled the *Tevaram* hymns sung in Tamil Nadu temples. This and the stylised Turuvaimozhi hymns for *Araiyar Sevai* [11], could be seen as parallel traditions. The term, *Sopanam*, in Sanskrit means step (*padi*, in the vernacular), according to Leela Omcheri, and refers to a musical ladder in which each note of the ascending and descending scales becomes a resting point, the singing eddying round the note till it moves to the next point. With no fixed scale or *shadja* as the starting point, *Sopanam*, in its reconstruction, is rendered in slowly increasing speed. The *Tali Nangyar*, it will be remembered, made her oblations perched on a step leading to the altar. The *Marars* who have now taken

Dancer Bharati Shivaji emotes the many moods of love.
Following pages 104-105: Dancer Vijayalakshmi brings out the exquisite grace and the difficult-to-acquire simplicity of the classical form in two movements from *nritta*.
Following page 106: Pallavi Krishnan in the form of the pensive maiden.
Following page 107: An eloquent look from Neetu Nair.

over the role earlier performed by the *Nangyar* are known as *Padiyilar*[12].

Kavalam Narayana Panikar and others have worked hard at making the contemporary music for Mohini Attam completely regional. Neither very slow like the theatre music for Kathakali nor like the stylised ritualistic music for traditions like *Mudiyettu* evoking the awesome aspect of Bhagavati, the music for Mohini Attam suits the '*Sukumara roopa*' or enticing nature of the dance.

The movement geometry and main technique of Mohini Attam reflects indelible images from the geography of Kerala: coconut fronds swaying in the breeze, boats bobbing, the waters patterned with ripples in concentric circles. It is a constant source of spiralling, uncoiling energy like the gradual awakening of the Kundalini Sakti (the latent energy) snaking up the spine. In the circling eddies of water there is no point marking the beginning or the end. It is the churning of the ocean that caused Mohini's appearance – she came from the same waters where Vishnu lies in utter repose, on his coiled snake bed. All these images seem to unite in Mohini Attam with its smooth circular movement of the torso forming the central motif. The flexibility of waist, shoulders, elbows and wrists operates within the measured discipline of the *andolika*, and is not to be exaggerated. Movement starts at the centre of the body and travels to the periphery or starts from the periphery to end at the centre. Along with the swaying torso is the lower half of the body in the half-seated posture with the out-turned knees, the formation more a square than a triangle. But, there is no consensus among dancers of the distance between the two feet. Eye movements, while not as exaggerated as in Kathakali, are vital. Elegance and dignity mark the pure white costume with a gold border, the tailored attire replacing the nine-yard *saree* in vogue thirty-five to forty years ago.

Kerala temples too are inspired by the circular motif, having rounded edges unlike the awesome verticality and etched lines of Tamil Nadu temples. The same aesthetic is reflected in the severely linear treatment of its dance. In Mohini Attam, it is the torso *andolika*, which responds to the curves in the music. The *Edekka* percussion instrument used in Mohini Attam is called the singing drum, its vocabulary of mnemonics or *vaitaris* like *takutein, tikutein, takukuteinkuku* having the same rounded softness in sound, unlike the etched crispness of Bharatanatyam *Sollus* or Kathak *Bols*.

Contemporary Mohini Attam is a polished version with changes wrought over time. The initial gurus were male. When Kalamandalam set up its Mohini Attam wing, Guru Krishna Panikkar had in the repertoire a truncated *Varnam*, *Padam*, and items like *Rasakrida* and *Gopi-vastrapaharanam* much like the *Krishnattam* tradition and the ensemble dances *Kaikottikali* and *Tiruvadirakkali*. The footwork had elements of *Tullal*, *Padayani* and *Arjunanrittam*. Kalyani Amma, one of the early teachers of Kalamandalam (around 1933-34), presented a *Tarana*-like number, which she called *Hindustani*. Kalpuratte Kunjukuttyamma, who in the early twentieth century trained under a host of teachers-Gopala Panikkar, Kunjan Panikkar, Krishna Menon and Puliyankotte Achyutan Nair-performed a *saree* dance as a prelude to the *Varnam*. Tottacheri Chinnammu Amma, known for her grace, Thankamani (who later married Mohini Attam Guru Gopinath) and many more dancers performed, but with no uniformity of style.

When the late Kalyanikuttyamma was persuaded by Vallattol to take to Mohini Attam, social prejudice against the dance was strong. After joining Kerala Kalamandalam in the 1930s, Kalyanikuttyamma had to stay away from her sister's marriage lest the groom's family get wrong ideas about the bride's family background. In 1940, after a quiet marriage to Kathakali maestro Krishnan Nair, Kalyanikuttyamma settled at Tripunithura, where the couple set up an institution in 1958. With her restrained *andolika* and expressional flair, Kalyanikuttyamma gave to Mohini Attam a Bharatanatyam precision, perhaps subconsciously – both daughters Sridevi and Kaladevi being trained Bharatanatyam dancers under Thanjavur Bhaskar Rao.

Mohini Attam dancers have strong views on the dance, reflected in their styles. Kerala Kalamandalam, in splendid isolation, has not accepted any style barring its own, even rejecting Kalyanikuttyamma's approach. With dancers like Kshemavathy, Sugandhi, Hymavathy, Saraswati, and K. Satyabhama, its creations have remained mostly in Kerala.

Mumbai-based dancer Kanak Rele claims to have rescued the dance from its sagging image with her work with scholars and dancers like Kunjukuttyamma and Chinnamuamma, both past their prime when she met them. She also runs Nalanda Research Centre, that combines dance training with a strong academic base, culminating in a post-graduate or/and doctoral degree.

With teachers like Madhaviamma and Krishna Panikkar having been with the Kerala Kalamandalam right from the 1930s, the dancer's claims are questioned.

Since pioneer Shanta Rao had been attracted enough by the dance to become a disciple of Krishna Panikkar, and Kalyaniyamma was sent to teach at Santiniketan (where she passed away) at the request of Rabindranath Tagore, the dance could not have been without aesthetic value. This in no way takes away from Kanaka Rele's contribution to Mohini Attam, with research assistance in libretto and music provided by Kavalam Narayana Panicker. A strong dancer, Rele's Mohini Attam inadvertently carries shades of the Kathakali energy, the dancer having undergone rigorous training under Guru Panchali Panikar for years. Her argument is that Panchali Panikar, famed for his *stree vesham*, had a soft femininity in his Kathakali, his dance in no way contraindicating the winsome grace called for in Mohini Attam.

Known for her graceful Mohini Attam, Bharati Sivaji in Delhi was a Bharatanatyam dancer for years before taking to this dance. Also assisted by Kavalam Narayana Panicker, she has enlarged the vocabulary by adapting movements from traditions like *Tullal*, *Kaikottikali*, *Tayambakam* and *Krishnattam*. Bharati Sivaji is inclined to think that Mohini Attam owes more to *Hastalakshanadipika*, while Kanak Rele would seem to consider that the dance finds early references in the *Balaramabharatam*. In her centre for Mohini Attam, Bharati has been training disciples. Interestingly, the inspirational base provided by Kavalam Narayana Panicker has created differently interpreted dance expressions by the two exponents.

Items like *Jiva*, *Tyanis*, Swati Tirunal *padams*, compositions of Irayaman Tampi, Cholkettu, Dandakam and several pieces of Kerala literature recently discovered by Leela Omcheri form the repertoire today. Kavalam's efforts have helped remove all the vestiges of the Dasiattam influence, if any.

Deepti Omcheri Bhalla at Delhi, with her combined music-dance expertise, has followed the controlled aesthetics and dignity of her guru Kalyanikuttyamma's style. But she has added many items through research assistance by her mother, musicologist Leela Omcheri[13]. Deepti's repertoire is entirely different, excepting for *Gita Govindam Ashtapadis*, which are common to all Mohini Attam presentations, each dancer interpreting the compositions in her way. Deepti tends to delve into *Tali Nangya* history for ideas, for she believes that the beginnings of Mohini Attam are to be found in the temple dancer of Kerala.

A dance based totally on entrancing grace, without the relief of rhythmic virtuosity, can be difficult to sustain before modern audiences with their notoriously short attention spans. Counter-pointing the dance *nayikas* exuding feminine grace, modern exponents have experimented with themes like '*Kubja* (hunch back) and Gandhari – the latter on a bitterly angry *Mahabharata* princess married off to a blind prince without prior knowledge. While these themes have inspired Kanak Rele, Bharati Sivaji and daughter Vijayalakshmi have produced a dance drama on a legendary princess Unniarchi who becomes a martial art expert, the work juxtapositioning Mohini Attam and Kalaripayattu.

In Kerala, where the dance is looked at from the perspective of the repertoire, the government has introduced Mohini Attam competitions in schools and colleges. This has swelled the numbers of dancers but not improved average standards. Experiments are not viewed encouragingly. But Kerala seems to be the only state where the classical dance repertoire of *Padams* is being recorded through a simple yet effective notation system evolved by scholar G. Venu.

To arrive at some consensus on stylistic aspects, pan-Indian seminars were held by organisations like Kerala Sangeet Natak Akademi (1968), with a workshop at Trishoor in 1990. A similar effort was mounted by Kalyanikuttyamma (1989) followed by Kanaka Rele and Bharati Sivaji with no significant change: all the main artistes ended up reiterating their views.

In more ways than one, this many-sided approach to the dance is not to be scoffed at for it saves the form from stereotypical uniformity, giving it vitality through multiple ideas.

In pockets, Mohini Attam has made itself felt on the international scene. As early as 1959, Betty Jones, an American, joined Kalamandalam to learn the dance and research it. Her monogram for the University of Pennsylvania is one of the very old records of the dance. At Melbourne (Australia), Tara Rajkumar, a Kathakali-Mohini Attam dancer who trained under great names like Guru Krishnan Nair and Kalyanikuttyamma, runs the successful *Natya Sudha*, training diaspora Indians and Australians in both styles.

Manipuri

Though it shares the philosophy of Indian classical dance, Manipuri is completely different in its visual manifestation. No hand and leg stretches give movement amplitude and spread, no foot contact rhythm articulates *tala* beats and no defined *mudra* or symbol registers a starting or finishing point. Instead it is a highly internalised art expression, seemingly easy but calling for years of disciplined training. In the continuous flow of movement, a photograph of a Manipuri dancer in action can recall no precise point. Unlike the plie with the sideway knee deflection common to all dances barring Kathak, the knees in Manipuri are bent forward. The dips and elevations of the dancer's body create a springy grace, the face indicating no emotion except serenity. Contrary to all Indian dances in which the body weight falls on the floor, the Manipuri dancer lifts weight off the floor, with feet gliding on and off it, a lyrical rhythm-in-the-air achieved without stomping. This highly contained artistry of movement is accompanied by high-pitched, intense music sung by throbbing soprano voices.

Intricately woven with the lifestyle of an Indo-Mongoloid stock of people, Manipuri is an indispensable part of religious worship. It heralds major events at home, like birth, marriage and even marks a death ceremony. The strong Vaishnavite superstructure of the dance is erected on the foundation of ancient rituals and animistic worship of a people who danced in meditative concentration to an abstract design symbolising an intertwined serpent and evoking a divinity unlike that of any known Hindu god. Accommodating ancient modes of worship with later Vaishnavite philosophy, Manipuri is both the oldest and the youngest of our dances.

Much of the old historical data of the region is lost, though the royal chronicles, the *Cheitharol Kumbaba* that Manipuris swear by, mention two pre-historic migrations to this land: one from the east, called *Nongpok Haram*; and the other from the west, called *Nongchup Haram*. The ethnologically complex land comprises the *Ningthouja* people who merged with the valley's clans to form a homogenous group, the *Meities*, a name by which they are still known thought they trace their antiquity to the Vedic age. Though the influence of the *Bhakti* movement was felt earlier, Vaishnavism was formally established about the eighteenth century. The most significant manifestation of ancient ritual is in the festival of *Lai Haraoba* or Celebration of the Gods

still enthusiastically observed. Old texts like the *Leithak-leikha-rol, Thirel-layat, Pudil* and *Panthoibi Khongul,* in archaic Manipuri, provide interesting insights into ancient belief. Living in nothingness, God *Athiya Guru Seedaba* created another entity *Aseeba,* whom he ordered to create the universe by first drawing out the gods and goddesses residing inside his mouth. *Aseeba* was not equal to the task, so *Seedaba* created an illusion of Himself which the gods faithfully followed chanting *Hoi*. The fragment comes from the term *Laihoilauba*[1] , which became *Lai Haraoba*. To mitigate the results of constant destruction (creation without destruction could have no meaning), God also created *Nongthang Laima,* a Mohini-like enchantress to tilt the balance in favour of the creative forces. Performed before *Lainingthou* (God) and *Lairemb*i (Goddess *Lairemma* in archaic Manipuri) in the open space or *Laibung* in every village, *Lai Haraoba* enacts the drama of creation. It also depicts scenes of romancing gods and of mundane acts like building thatched huts, growing cotton, weaving and fishing.

The entire community participates in the festival conducted by the *Maibas,* high priests, with specialised dances by *Maibis,* a class of high priestesses (*maibi* can also be male). Women (or men, in rare instances) suddenly showing unusual emotional behaviour are taken to the *Imam Maibi* (Mother Maibi) who, after assuring herself of genuine indications of a *Maibi*-to-be, initiates the person, putting her through rigorous training in dance and music. There is no bar on a *Maibi* marrying and having children. In *Lai Haraoba*, singers playing the *Pena,* the traditional single-stringed instrument, awaken the gods in *Lai-yakaiba*. In *Laiching-Jagoi,* a *Maibi* summons the deity. The morning ritual, *Laimang Phamba*, has a *Maibi* chanting hymns till possessed by the divine spirits she turns into an oracle. *Laisem-Jagoi* portrays the creation of the earth, and the auspicious *Laiboung-Chongba,* resembling a dance anthology, traces the creation of the human body. It is rendered to the accompaniment of the lyrics of the *Anoirol,* played and sung by the *pena* player. The festival has numerous segments including *Panthoibi-Jagoi,* the amorous dance of God *Nongpok Ningthou* and Goddess *Panthoibi*[2]. Another sequence has dancers moving to the abstract design of the *yumjao paphal,* a traditional snake pattern symbolising God *Pakhangba*. With processions and chants, the festival concludes with a formal ceremony of temple offerings. Over the years this festival has taken on three regional forms *Kanglei, Chakpa* [2a], and *Moirang.*

A moon-snake god and also the name of a King, *Pakhangba* was acknowledged king after he cleverly won an around-the-world race by circumambulating his father. The losing contestant, brother *Sanamahi,* the Sun God, was compensated by being made the presiding deity of every house, the southwest wing being regarded as the Sanamahi corner[3].

Tantric and Saivite strains too are part of the valley, itself believed to have been submerged in water sucked out by Siva's trident, enabling him to dance with Parvati.

Vaishnavism first came into the valley in the time of King Kyamba (1467-1508). The first Vishnu temple in the region is ascribed to King Khagemba (1630), while King Chairongba (1697-1708) was initiated into Acharya Nimbarkar's cult. His son Garib Nivas (1709-1748) is credited with introducing Vaishnavism into the region[4]. Religious reformers like Santi Dass, Madhavacharya, Vishnuswami, and Ramanandji left their impressions, their literature inspiring many a later Manipuri Guru. It was left to King Bhagyachandra (1763-1798) to make Gaudiya Vaishnavism the state religion. He is also believed to have conceived of the *Manipuri Raasa* dances in a religious trance.

Apart from Bhagyachandra's immense contribution to Manipuri dance, kings like Nara Singh, Gambhir Singh, Chandrakirti, Chaurajit, and Surchandra were all art connoisseurs, some even dancers. The *Mridanga-Saranga* with its fund of information on percussion rhythms was the legacy of Chandrakirti. The kings introduced expert academies or *Loisangs* that looked after *Raasa* and *Sankirtan*. These still exist, though in a diminished form, as the final authority on all matters relating to the dancer.

Manipuri festivals like *Krishna Janma, Radha Janma, Jhoolan Yatra, Rath Yatra* [4a], *Jalakheli,* and *Hari Utthan* [4b] revolve round the Krishna myth. While dance and music were always part of worship, Vaishnavism introduced special *mandaps* (pavilions) for the performance of *Raasa,* unlike in *Lai Haraoba* where a meeting of the earth and the sky is ideally enacted in the open. Nowhere is the Krishna-Gopi *Raasa* interaction of the *Bhagavat Purana* as meticulously translated into the dance as in Manipuri. Performed entirely by women with Krishna's role too taken by a

female dancer, this dance theatre is a unique blend of splendour and devotion. Bhagyachandra's contribution includes *Vasanta Raasa*, rendered on the Holi full moon day, *Kunja Raasa* during the full moon of *Rakhi Poornima,* and *Maha* Raasa on *Kartik Poornima.* Chandrakirti introduced *Nitya Raasa* and *Gopa Raasa,* each built round an episode from *Bhagavat Purana. Diva Raasa* introduced by Chuda Chang is the only *Raasa* performed during the day. *Raasa* is first performed in the Govindji shrine in Imphal before being presented in *khulak* (village) temples.

Raasa in Manipur is a never-to-be-forgotten experience of aesthetics and devotional fervour. Every minute detail, from the designing and decoration of the pavilion to the orderly seating of the official overseers and audience, even to the folding of a betel leaf or the cutting of the areca nut into shapes, is guided by sensitivity and an eye for precision and discipline. Preparation protocol starts five days earlier with chants propitiating the gods and the pavilion being washed and covered with straw mats *(phaks).* In the Govindji temple, the ceremonially escorted statues of Radha (made of gold) and Krishna are installed on the rotating wooden dais in the *Mandap* centre[5]. Starting after the evening prayers, the performance ends with prayers next

morning. The circular geometry of the dance in a square *Mandap* symbolises the meeting point of the macro and the micro, of the heavenly and the earthly. The circular formation represents the *Mandala* with concentric circles within. *Raasa* also symbolises the seasonal cycle. The metrical cycles to which movement is rendered represents yet another circle. With the gorgeously sequined, *zari*-embroidered, stiff lower skirt *(Kumin)* and the transparent folds of the upper skirt *(Poshuwan)* also moving with the dancer's *Bhramaris* (pirouettes), the audience is lost in a world of spinning delight and devotion[6]. Formations like *Hallisaka, Pindibandha*, and *Charchari* that are mentioned in the *Natya Sastra* are best expressed in the Manipuri *Raasa.*

The auspicious prologue to the *Raasa,* the *Purvarang* as it is called, is the *Sankirtan,* an independent artistic ritual of ecstatic singing, dancing and rhythm-keeping in praise of Radha and Krishna. Closely associated with the eight *sanskaras* of a life cycle, this elaborate form of community prayer comprises male drummers and cymbal players *(Nata-Pala).* The women performers *(Nupi-Pala),* wielding smaller cymbals called *Mandila,* are assigned to festivals like *Jalakheli* and *Durga Puja.* Some celebrations are only practised by royal houses: *Raseswari,* for example, is rendered only by women hailing from the Raja Bhagyachandra line.

Male and female roles in Manipuri are distinct. The Manipuri *tandav* dancer keeps the two feet apart at a specified four *talas*, unlike the *lasya* in which the feet are held close. Feline leaps and jumps *(achongba)*; raising a foot as high as the calf, the knee or even the thigh; and jumping and spiralling in the seated position with knees and feet close together[7] are seen. *Nata Pala* comprises the *Cholom* dances in which dancers/percussionists move to rhythms played on the *Pung* drum and the *Kartal* (cymbals). Designed to ritualistically worship Radha and Krishna, the rhythm rises to a crescendo to signify union and then drops. This constant ebb and tide of energy is central to the fine toned rhythm-dance weave. Less robust than *Pung Cholom*, *Kartal Cholom* is the embodiment of grace and balance. The male dancer's ability to emulate the gait of the elephant, the deer, the snake, and the swan [8] is part of the training. Tonal variations in cymbal playing can also evoke sounds like that of rumbling thunder or of gentle rain. Only in *Rath Yatra* does rhythm take on a clipped hand-clapping *(Khubak Isei)* form, crisply articulating individual units of time, unlike the flowing resonance of *Kartal* rhythm.

Alongside is the devotional ecstasy marking the singing of *Sankirtan Padavalis* beginning with a homage to Chaitanya Mahaprabhu. There is no attempt at translating the hymn through gesture or movement. The entire *Pala,* comprising two main *Pung* players (*Pung-Yeibas*) with a semi-circle round them of the *Kartal* players, moves either clockwise or semi-clockwise. One of the most versatile percussion instruments, the *Pung,* has an astonishing tonal range; the *Pung Raga*, a percussion prologue, being a test of professional expertise. Percussion instruments like the *Dholak, Dhol, Dafat,* and *Khanjari* are integral to *Holi Sankirtan* in Manipur. Manipuri has its own conventions in the host of *talas* constituting the rhythmic vocabulary. The synchronicity of Manipuri dancing and drumming has been developed to a nicety.

Immaculate, snow-white, *dhoti*-clad dancers – their *Pung* slung in front, a white top cloth gracefully draped over the left shoulder covering part of the *Pung* – perform in perfect group discipline, throwing off the elegant white turban in unison with one graceful nod of the head, the fallen turbans making a neat flower-like row on the floor.

Apart from cross rhythms, the metrical cycle has

unarticulated fractional punctuations, with silent hand play in the air. The *lasya* aspect limits movement to space close to the body, with the knees held close together and no sharp bends. But, there is a constant change of vertical levels, the dancer weaving a figure of '8' with her entire body [10], with each movement flowing into the next. The hands too, tracing a graceful figure of '8' with loosely held fingers, are guided by understated aesthetics and containment.

The *Chali* in Manipuri with which all training starts is done to a time measure of eight beats (*Tanchep tal*). The *Bhangi-parengs* are cadences of movement with varying body flexions, the *Tandava* and *Lasya Bhangi-parengs* being different. The *lasya* part often uses a starting sideways movement followed by a semi-circle on the right and then the left, called *uplai* and *longlai* respectively. Male performers of *Jagoi* (dance) occasionally use this movement, not, however, found in *Nata Pala* or *Cholom*

Singing in Manipur goes with the dance and, while occasionally resembling some of the melodic modes of the Hindustani and Carnatic traditions, is completely different in its microtonal treatment. Voice production of the high tremelo and soprano type, the trills and yodels and the deliberately cracked voice in parts have a distinct character, the high pitch endowing it with a throbbing power. The singing accompanying a scene of *Vasaka Sajja* (the woman waiting for her beloved) rendered at night can create an emotional storm within the audience.

Geographical isolation with a prevailing sense of ethnological separateness has been a feature of Manipur. While insulating art traditions from globalisation, this has led to less interaction with the rest of India's performing arts. Manipuri became known to the rest of India only when Rabindranath Tagore in 1919 was treated to a *Raasa* performance for the first time in the Sylhet district (now in Bangladesh). He arranged forthwith to have the dance taught in Santiniketan by recruiting Gurus Mahakumar and Buddhimanta from Tripura. Centres of Manipuri training came into being in Ahmedabad, Kolkata, and Shillong. With Tagore's abiding interest, well-known impresario Haren Ghosh toured the country with a Manipuri troupe in 1930, putting the dance form on the all-India map.

Three great gurus Amubi Singh, Amudon Sharma, and Atomba Singh were associated with the twentieth-

century Manipuri scene. Guru Priya Gopal Sena heading the Jawaharlal Nehru Manipur Dance Academy, Imphal, for years as principal produced the acclaimed dance work, *Bhagyachandra*. Amongst notable female artistes is the inimitable Thambal Devi. Some of the Sankirtan greats, Gambhini Devi and Thoranisabi Devi, carved a niche for themselves as singers of tremendous vitality performing *abhinaya* of rare vintage. Guru Amubi Singh's epoch making contribution to Manipuri comprised a repertoire of solo and group compositions. The prestigious Jawaharlal Nehru Manipur Dance Academy at Imphal started in 1955 by the Central Sangeet Natak Akademi follows his style of Manipuri. Dancers from this institution rank among the best. Guru Amubi Singh also taught at Uday Shankar's Almora Centre. Among his many disciples is the erudite Guru Rajkumar Singhajit Singh, heading the Manipuri faculty of Triveni Kala Sangam, Delhi, for years. He has fashioned several productions on secular and mythological themes, conceived in association with his wife, the well-known Manipuri dancer, Charu Sija Mathur[11].

Guru Amudon Sharma's disciple the late Guru Bipin Singh trained several students in his Kolkata institution, Manipur Nartanalaya, that has a Mumbai branch. A far more extroverted dance expression than Guru Amubi Singh's, Bipin Singh's Manipuri was guided more by proscenium compulsions. Undeterred by criticism of taking the dance away from its traditional confines with the feet clad in ankle bells, and the crisp foot-contact-rhythm accenting syllables, Guru Bipin Singh, who had his battles with the Manipur dance establishment, remained till the end an individualist, looking at the dance his own way. Translating his ideas on the stage were his disciples, the Jhaveri Sisters of whom only Darshana Jhaveri is active. His compositions included works like *Anangakshep* for the solo dancer, and many dance drama compositions based on Tagore's works. *Rabindra Sangeet* with its slow cadence, according to him, suited the Manipuri body language [12].

Manipuri, still so closely linked with the temple, has found the proscenium sensibility challenging. 'No matter what one may do, there is no God on the stage,' says a Sankirtan exponent, 'and while trying to evoke the same presence, I feel different.' This response reaffirms that what is done for the proscenium while different from what constitutes ritual can be an aesthetic delight in disciplined artistry.

A dance mainly based on group energy has now acquired a solo dimension comprising sequences from within *Raasa,* and interpretative dance based on *Padavalis* and *Ashtapadis*. Guru Amubi Singh himself had anticipated the solo compulsions. But unless rendered by seasoned dancers, the solo from the *Raasa* traditionally presented in the group backdrop, can seem limp. The full impact of Manipuri lyricism and understated aesthetics without the exuberantly articulated virtuosity of other dance forms is often lost on uninitiated audiences. And the dance sadly does not enjoy the frequent platforms other classical dances attract. Barring pockets in the east of the country and in Mumbai, Manipuri is still largely confined to its environs[13]. Non-proliferation also has advantages: with Manipuri too much has not led to too little by diluting standards with mediocrity. For the *Sankirtan* exponents, who are much in demand for various ceremonies in Manipur, lack of proscenium space matters little. It is the *Raasa* performer who really feels the pinch of insufficient performance opportunities.

Folk, classical, and martial art forms like *Thang Ta* of Manipur present a wide vocabulary of movement that can be explored creatively. A disciple of Atomba Singh and the late Guru Amubi Singh, Chaotombi Singh of Jawaharlal Nehru Manipur Dance Academy, choreographed a dance drama, *Sangai.* based on director Aribam Syam Sharma's *Keibul Lamjaol.* The theme was the decimation of the dancing deer of Manipur. The pioneering work made waves in the dance world, its poignant ecological statement drawing its movement vocabulary from tribal, folk, martial art and classical dance. The other person to have effectively experimented with the rich vocabulary of movement is Ratan Thiyam, the highly talented theatre director, whose work *Chakravyuha*, with its stunningly powerful images of movement, has created theatre history. *Thang Ta*, the martial art, has attracted many choreographers though their endeavours rest as scattered work.

Still, the tradition, as a vital part of the lives of the people of Manipur, is strong.

Kuchipudi

The growth of Kuchipudi in the last half century is one more instance in post-Independence India of a little known local tradition – practised by Brahmin performers of an Andhra Pradesh village – spreading to all parts of India, acquiring a large following, with its tone and presentation undergoing substantial changes in the process. The Kuchipudi scene today bristles with a majority of female exponents in what was once an all-male tradition.

The story of the dance in its present form starts about sixteenth century A.D. though architectural evidence from the second-century B.C. Amaravati Stupa with carvings of group dancing (*pindibandha*) and Nagarjuna sculptures suggest dance was a popular pastime. From the eleventh century, dance references are found in treatises like *Saraswati Hridayalankara* by Nandydeva, *Manasollasa* by Someswara, *Sangeeta Chudamani* by Pratapa Cakravarti and *Sanjita Parijata* by Ahola (1600 A.D.). Significantly, the thirteenth-century *Nrittaratnavali* by Jayappa Senani, a reputed scholar and dancer who was Commander of the Elephant Forces of the Kakatiya ruler, Ganapati Deva, mentions *Brahmana mela*. Similar traditions like *Pagativeshalu* and *Bahurupalu* (the last also mentioned in Palkuriki Somanatha's *Panditaradhya charita*), where the actor appeared in varied guise, were prevalent amongst the actors of Gaddipaddu, a Brahmin settlement (*agraharam*). Historical evidence for Kuchipudi is in the Manchupalli Kaifiat of 1502 A.D., which refers to a *Bhagavatulu* group obtaining audience with the ruler of Vijayanagar, Immadi Narasimha Nayaka, and successfully conveying through their dance drama the message of victimisation under the local chieftain Sammeta Guruva Raju of Siddhavatam. Raju was consequently removed. The other evidence pertains to a yet untraced copper plate which records the granting of a Kuchipudi village by the Nawab of Golkonda, Abdul Hasan Tani Shah, who ruled from 1672 to1687 A.D., to *Bhagavatulu* families in appreciation of their art after witnessing their dance drama on a visit to Machilipatnam.

The missing copper plate grant and the presence of more than one village named Kuchipudi make conclusive proof of the village which has come to be recognised as the repository of the *Bhagavatulu* dance being the very one granted by Hasan Tani Shah difficult. A property division document, allocating (24 August

1763) shares in a Kuchipudi village mentions fifteen families[1] of which at least half a dozen are actively involved with the dance today. The document mentions that old *sanads* and records are lost, but is silent about the village being a grant by the ruler to the people.

Near Vinukonda, another Kuchipudi village was known for its itinerant group of Brahmin performers famous for *Kelika* (play), for *Keertana* (musical performance) and for impersonating characters. Yet another Kuchipudi in Tenali Taluq (a dance village is in Divi Taluq of Krishna district) that had a vibrant tradition of Kuchipudi has two temples of Ramalingaswamy and Gopalaswamy, the hereditary priests here hailing from the Vedantam and the Pasumarthi families of Kuchipudi, now in the other village. Marital alliances between various Brahmin *agraharam* families were common and at some point all Kuchipudi activity may have shifted to the Divi Taluq village.

Etymologically, the term *Kuchipudi* which stood for female dancers became *Potu kuchu* (a male dancer) and, finally, came to mean Brahmin dancer. Pudi[2] is a term applied to a village built over accumulated alluvial soil. There are other far-fetched theories[3], Sanskritologists even inferring that the term Kuchipudi is a corruption of *Kuchelapuram*, the village of a poor Brahmin friend of Lord Krishna in a myth.

The *Bhakti* movement had its most eloquent expression in the *Natya melam*, where dance troupes presented musical plays on Vaishnavite themes on makeshift stages in what was known as *Veedi Natakam* (street theatre). While the learning and Sanskrit knowledge required by the Kuchipudi actor are cited as having dictated the Brahmin emphasis, it is clear the art form acquired its character because of the nature of the performers who came from a Sanskrit background. The Kuchipudi *Bhagavatulu* specialised not only in dance drama or *Yakshagana* but also in a special category of opera called *Kalapams*. *Kalapams* were a form of total theatre interwoven with a structure of musical compositions called *Daru-s*, all relating to one theme. *Bhama Kalapam*, portraying the mercurial Satyabhama, a consort of Krishna, in her diverse moods is Kuchipudi's piece de resistance. To excel in this role is the highest goal of a dancer. *Golla Kalapam*, the other popular opera, is a dialogue between a sagacious milkmaid and a *brahmin*, on the philosophy of life from 'womb to tomb', the exchange laced with metaphysical statements, poetry, and humour. These plays and the dance drama *Parijatapaharanam* have been attributed to Siddhendra Yogi, the legendary preceptor of Kuchipudi, though there are many versions of this play composed at different times by unspecified authors. No historical evidence on Siddhendra, assigned to different periods from the fourteenth to the seventeenth century, exists. Some even trace him to Melattur in Tanjore district, from where he is said to have migrated to Kuchipudi. He is described as an orphan brought up by kindly neighbours who also arranged his marriage. Siddhendra was saved by divine intervention from certain death by drowning while he was trying to cross a river in spate as he was returning from Udipi, where he had gone on a learning pursuit. True to his promise to the Lord, he became an ascetic, singing and dancing the praises of Lord Vishnu. He is credited with having got the Kuchipudi village gifted to the Bhagavatulu. Even if Siddhendra, whose name occurs but once[4] in a very old *Bhama Kalapam* manuscript, did indeed contribute to the dance, he did not create it. Precursors like *Baintaveshams* and *Aataveshams* were popular with the Bhagavatulu families. *Kalapams* were presented outside the temple precincts for public entertainment, also by the *devadasis* known as *bhogamvaru* or *saanulu*. Their librettos had a heroine-centric treatment emphasising the development of the *nayika* rather than the Vaishnavite missionary message of the Bhagavatulu. The *Yakshagana* as a form of presentation goes back to old times; out of it rose the *Mahanatakams* or grand plays written by the Nayaka rulers of Tanjore like Vijayaraghava Nayaka (1633-1672 A.D.) who composed *Parijatapaharanam*. One Mukku Timanna, court poet of Vijayanagar emperor Krishnadeva Raya, had earlier written a work on the same theme.

The other great name in Kuchipudi after Siddhendra Yogi, Narayana Tirtha also wrote *Parijatam* – but for the Melattur Bhagavata Mela Natakam performers, who were a break-off from the *Bhagavatulu* of Andhra Pradesh and had migrated to Tanjore after the battle of Talakota in 1565 A.D. (*see Bharatanatyam chapter*). Narayana Tirtha's work clearly mentions the Tanjore village of Achyutapuram where the *Bhagavatulu* were settled[5]. Unlike their counterpart in Kuchipudi, the *Mela Natakam* tradition was not an itinerant one, but remained localised in villages like Melattur, Saliyamangalam, Oothukadu and Soolamangalam.

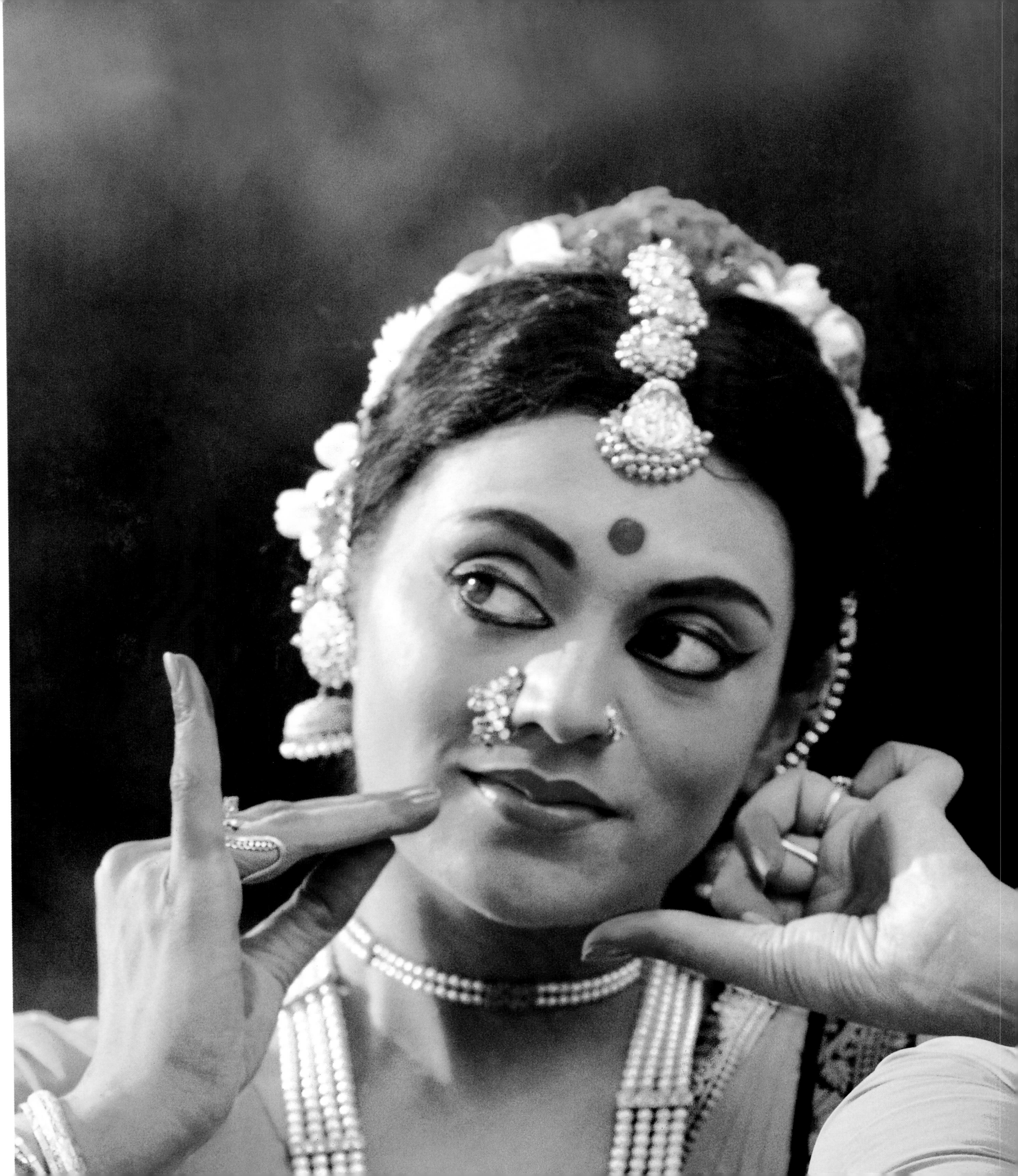

127

Abhinaya comes to the fore
as dancer Swapnasundari
essays two stylised poses.

Narayana Tirtha's marathon Sanskrit musical composition *Krishna Leela Tarangini* occupies prime place in the Kuchipudi repertoire. Comprising 153 *Keertanams* (lyrics of a specific structure), 302 *Slokams* (verses of praise for the Gods, 30 *Darus* (a special structure of musical composition) and innumerable *gadya* or prose passages, the work was a milestone in literature and art. Conceived in a multiplicity of rare melodic modes, the *Tarangini* covered the gamut of childhood representations and Lord Krishan's romantic interactions with the *gopis*.

Darus, a specifically structured composition used in different situations to establish a character in the play, are a prominent part of the musical text for Kuchipudi. *Natya Abhishekha Sabdams* in praise of deities and royalty, contributed by poets like Veerabhadraiyya and by Melattur poets like Kasinathaiyya and Venkatarama Sastry are all part of the Kuchipudi repertoire[6]. Being travelling actors, Kuchipudi artistes gathered ideas and compositions from different areas. For instance, the nineteenth-century actor Hari Madhavaiyya is said to have borrowed librettos of some Melattur plays like *Prahlada charitam*, perhaps as a role model for composers of plays on similar themes in the Kuchipudi area. Despite the fact that plays on common themes are presented by both *Bhagavata Mela* and Kuchipudi actors, libretto and treatment, not to speak of the dance language, are very different.

Curiously, in what was an all-male tradition, female roles like those of Satyabhama, Rukmini, Usha, Mohini etc. were pre-eminent. *Streevesham* with its cross-gender impersonation carried much weight and the male as female was the main image associated with Kuchipudi identity in popular perception. A dancer like Vedantam Satyanarayana Sarma, famed for his portrayal of Satyabhama in *Bhama Kalapam*, does not allow the woman's identity to slip even while engaged in the mundane act of adjusting the microphone on the stage before commencing the famous *lekha* scene in *Bhama Kalapam*. The scene portrays Satyabhama as she writes a love letter to her consort Krishna in the most poetic language. The role of the actor in Kuchipudi included spoken bits of dialogue and even sung passages. This comprehensive singing, acting, and dancing prowess of the performer has now been changed to a largely dance-oriented expertise. The vocalist in the team of musicians accompanying the performance has taken

over all the singing. As for the dialogue passages in Telugu, they have become rare among urban dancers coming from a variety of backgrounds. Only in the traditional *Yakshagana* presentation by the village troupes does one get to hear the spoken passages. The only exception in the contemporary scene of a dancer who can sing, speak and dance the *Kalapams* is Swapnasundari. She has probed the Andhra *devadasi* solo tradition and worked at reconstructing the dance, now called *Vilasini Natyam*, with research assistance provided by the late Dr Arudra.

In Kuchipudi, the movement does not have one central stance round which the technique revolves. The half-seated position with the knees flexed sideways is much used, but not as the main stylistic concern as in Bharatanatyam. But, movements are repeated on both sides of the body as in Bharatanatyam. There is a springy graceful up and down movement, with the dancer constantly changing levels with frequent weight shifts – the foot-contact continually changing with flat feet touching the floor or heels, toes and even the side of the feet tapping the floor. Moving forward with the big toe of the two feet interlocked is a typical gait, as is executing rhythm patterns in the crossed feet position. A very vigorous and pacy dance form, Kuchipudi has little use for the savoured slowness of pace seen in others. Even the interpretative parts are not leisurely in tempo. The lilt and metre of poetry and song are invariably catchy and invest the dance with a quicksilver vibrancy. The dance-music relationship is less structured than in other dances and often a one-line repetitive musical backdrop as in *Krishna Sabdam* and *Tarangam*, which provides a lilt and emphasises a mood, sees the dancer presenting an entire narrative sequence or canvas of mime and rhythm woven into the *tala* cycle. The dancer's jaunty stride as she enters the stage and makes her exit in a quick graceful goose step, the tip of the long decorated braid held in the left hand is characteristic of Kuchipudi. The walk has an air of saucy grace and sensuous appeal. The character in a traditional play is introduced from behind a curtain (*tera*) held by two persons on either side – a practice that in solo dance is followed only in *Bhama Kalapam*, in which the only visible part of the dancer is the braid flung over the curtain. The braid (*jada*)[7] challenges anyone in the audience to try and equal the dancer's prowess.

While not much is recorded of ancient Kuchipudi

actors, the names of the nineteenth-century Hari Madhavaiyya, and of his able disciples Chinta Venkatratnam and brother Chinta Venkatramaiyya (1860-1949) are known. Tadepalli Peraiyya Sastry (1886-1942), the main guru of Vempati Chinna Satyam who learnt later under Lakshminarayana Sastri too, is said to have often deputised as the *Sutradhar* (narrator) and *Vidhushaka* (jester) in the *Atta Bhagavatams* presented by the *devadasis*, proving the interaction between the two parallel traditions. Solo Kuchipudi where unconnected items (some of them independent sequences from longer plays) formed the concert presentation by a single dancer, was started by Guru Vedantam Lakshminarayana Sastry (1875 – 1957) who also taught *devadasis*. His fame spilled beyond the Kuchipudi arena, with dancers from other schools – like Balasaraswati, Gowri Ammal, Ram Gopal and Tara Chowdhury – seeking him out in his Ramanujam Street home in Chennai. The main Guru of Vempati Chinna Satyam, he also trained C. R. Acharyalu, who became the Kuchipudi guru for Mrinalini Sarabhai's Darpana Academy at Ahmedabad. Lakshminarayana also trained Nataraj Ramakrishna, who reconstructed some old performance traditions of *devadasis*, like *Nava Janardhana Parijatham* categorised under *Andhra Natyam*. In appreciation of his services, Lakshminarayana Sastry was presented a *Simhatalatamu* (carved gold bracelet) when he was 68, the function at Chennai having a female dancer Samrajyam doing the *Balagopala Tarangam*. The *Tarangam* (a display of virtuosity: the dancer weaves intricate rhythm patterns with the feet planted on the rim of a brass plate) was started by Lakshminarayana Sastry as an audience-pleasing device.

Despite Gurus like Chinta Narayanamurthy, Yeleswaroopa Narayanappa, Vedantam Raghavaiya, Chinta Venkatramayya and Lakshminarayana Sastry being famed for *stree vesham*, women dancers had begun to enter the portals of Kuchipudi. In fact, an article by late Mohan Khokar[8] records how at the awards function for Lakshminarayana Sastry, the then Finance Minister B. Gopala Reddy declared in his speech that Kuchipudi had no future unless women were inducted into the dance.

Caste barriers had crumbled. At Nuzvid, C. R. Acharyalu trained Korada Narasimha Rao who came from outside the traditional Kuchipudi family. He was

later trained by Lakshminarayana Sastry also and became famous for the vigour of demon roles like that of Bhasmasura, cast in a rough-hewn mould. Korada Narasimha Rao joined as the male partner of the late Indrani Rehman, already an established Bharatanatyam dancer, and the two set a trend for male-female duets, still very popular in Kuchipudi which is full of husband and wife duos: Raja and Radha Reddy, Narasimhachary and Vasantha Lakshmi, Vanashree and Jayarama Rao and other *lasya-tandava* couple groupings, not necessarily of man and wife.

Two female dancers, Mohana and Samanti performed Kuchipudi in Mumbai in 1955, when, even in the Sangeet Natak Akademi National Dance Festival, Kuchipudi was listed as 'Kuchipudi-Bharatanatyam'. Barring a short demonstration by one Kanchanamala, there was no other slot for this dance even in the 1958 Sangeet Natak Akademi Festival featuring obscure forms. In a peeve, the Andhra Pradesh Sangeet Akademi in 1959 mounted a seminar with learned papers contributed by Banda Kanakalingeswara Rao, Ayyanki Tandava, Lanka Suryanarayana Sastry and Ramakottaiya to support the case of Kuchipudi being recognised as a classical dance form. Branches of the reputed Siddhendra Kalakshetra at Kuchipudi village were set up at Elluru and Gudivala. Nataraj Ramakrishna's *Yakshagana* production of *Kumara Sambhavam* and Sampatkumar's *Abhijnana Sakuntalam* presented on the occasion convinced dance personalities like E. Krishna Iyer, Damayanti Joshi and Naina Jhaveri that Kuchipudi deserved to be brought under classical dance.

Dancers from non-traditional backgrounds like Raja and Radha Reddy began to set up flourishing schools. After Indrani Rehman, the next female practitioner to carry Kuchipudi to all corners of the globe was Yamini Krishnamurthy, whose *Bhama Kalapam* and *Krishna Sabdam* became the inevitable finale for almost all her dance recitals, so popular were they. Chinta Krishnamurthy, the Guru, had no compunction in saying that Yamini had given star status to Kuchipudi.

Kuchipudi village became too small to contain the widening horizon of the dance and many teachers gravitated to Chennai in search of a place in the vibrant film world. The dancers they dealt with were almost always female, and gone now were the mustachioed, strutting male characters of *Yakshagana* as Hiranyakashipu, Jarasandha, Bali and Bhasmasura –

135

Dancer Shobha Naidu depicts the *Viswaroopa*, the cosmic dimension of Lord Vishnu, in the dance drama *Shri Krishnam Sharanam Mama*.
Facing page: Hail Siva! Dancer Raja Reddy portrays the all-conquering Siva in the *Urdhva Tandava* pose.

except in the village. The urban manifestation of the dance saw even divine characters like Rama, Krishna and Srinivasa, now rendered by female dancers, develop a soft and gentle tone. Kuchipudi had come full circle.

Today, the man enacting a woman's role has become rare. Even veteran Vedantam Satyanarayana Sarma prefers to demonstrate *stree vesham* in normal male attire with only the face made up and the eyes accentuated with *kohl*. Son of late Guru Vedantam Rattaiyya Sarma, Vedantam Venkatachalapati is adept at female impersonation, which he combines with male roles, giving himself a wider choice unlike his famous uncle Satyanarayana Sarma who specialises only in female roles. Nataraj Ramakrishna in his revived Nava Janardhana Parijatham, a tradition of the old Pendele *devadasi* family of Pithapuram, has trained Kala Krishna, for performing Satyabhama's role – though the dance in its mixed Kuchipudi-folksy vibes comes under Andhra Natyam. Pasumarthy and Yeleswaroopa Srinivasan are among the males doing female roles. But with so many female dancers dominating the scene, there is little incentive for cross-gender impersonation.

With much Kuchipudi activity having shifted to urban areas, it is the village Sindhendra Kalakshetra, which now requires more muscle in terms of teachers and students. The sophisticated urban version of the dance owes a lot to Vempati Chinna Satyam and his Kuchipudi Art Academy at Chennai where a long line of now-established dancers have been trained. Most of them are running their own institutions in India and abroad: Shobha Naidu, Ratna Kumar, Kamala Reddy, Sasikala, Kalpalatika, Anuradha Nehru, Anuradha Jonnalgedda, Manju Bhargavi and the guru's own son, Vempati Ravi. Staging his large corpus of dance drama productions born out of years of collaboration with libretto specialist Bhujanga Sarma and musician P. Sangeetha Rao in every corner of the globe, Vempati has played no small role in putting Kuchipudi on the international map. An unabashed defender of female dancers doing even male roles, Chinna Satyam feels that the male in female roles is no longer relevant today. Music for Kuchipudi had not ventured beyond a handful of favourite ragas like *Mohanam, Mukhari, Bhairavi, Todi* and *Kamboji*, till Vempati began to harness a range of ragas – some unfamiliar even to Carnatic concert platforms – for his dance drama compositions. His conscious polishing of movement is sometimes

(Top) Guru Vempati Chinnasatyam doing *abhinaya*; (bottom) Following in the footsteps of the father, Vempati Ravi Shankar shows pure dance movements. *Facing page:* Dancer Mallika Sarabhai strikes two poses.

criticised as having made too glossily perfect a tradition deriving its vibrancy from a folk-like informality. The dancer's lip synchronisation with the words of the song that Vempati insists on, while followed by most dancers is not a feature all Kuchipudi teachers agree on. Chinna Satyam's style is undoubtedly the most widely prevalent today, though the Reddys, Jaya Rama Rao, Narasimhachary's, Swapnasundari and others have over the years evolved their own style, each having several productions to his or her credit. The approach to *abhinaya* is particularly varied. Nataraj Ramakrishna insists on *satvika abhinaya*, where totally internalised emotions are expressed through minimal but intense movement. Vempati makes the whole body (*angikaabhinaya*) express emotion. A dancer like Swapnasundari in the *devadasi* mode specialises in building a range of interpretations round each word of the song through gesture and facial expression. Between the traditional Kuchipudi in which one 'becomes a character' and the solo form where the performer as the narrator maintains an aesthetic distance from what he or she portrays, there is a subtle difference, often not entirely grasped by dancers who tend to over-dramatise solo non-representative presentation also.

The Reddys are the ultimate showmen, their presentation rarely matched by other dancers. In spite of its proliferation, Kuchipudi has been comparatively less threatened by change outside its parameters. The dance in interior Andhra Pradesh still enjoys a measure of privacy and troupes from there have less exposure on the international stage. Barring dance drama production based on Tagore's work, *Chandalika*, dealing with untouchability (by Vempati Chinna Satyam) or a Buddhist play like *Bhagavajjukiyam*, where transferred souls in exchanged bodies result in a monk acting like a courtesan and vice versa (produced by Raja Reddy), Kuchipudi has not been harnessed to daringly new themes. Visual attraction and rhythmic excitement are what it thrives on.

The best innovative use of the technique, while preserving its classical format, has been by Rama Bharadwaj, settled in the United States, in a production of *Panchatantra*. Clearly, as the dance gets involved in the wider international arena, it will be challenged in more ways.

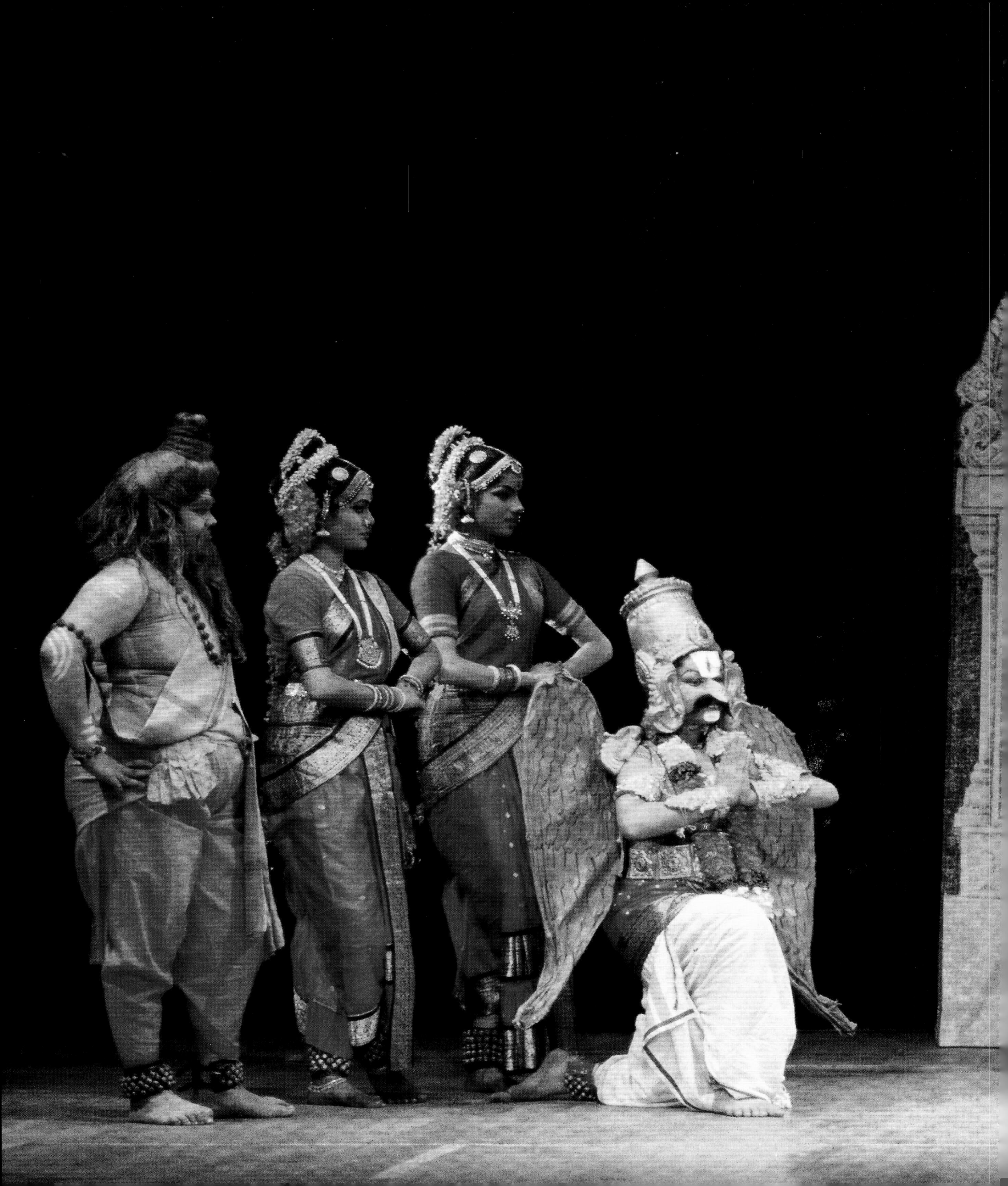

Footnotes

BHARATANATYAM

1 The anthologies are: Narrinai, Kuruntogai, Aingurunuru, Padirruppattu, Paripadal, Kalittogai, Ahanaanuru, Puranaanuru, and Pattuppattu.

2 *Arangetram*: a term that still prevails.

3 *Santi Kuttu*: The word has been used to indicate classical dance in inscriptions and literature.

4 A form of poetry the object of which is to conduct one to a superior.

5 Appar (Tirunavukkarasu), Sundarar, Sambandar and Manikkavachakar

6 For further details refer to Lakshmi Viswanathan's book, *Bharatanatyam -Tamil heritage.*

7 In the hundred and thousand pillared halls in the temples of Chidambaram, Kumbakonam, Tiruvizhimizhalai, on the *kantha* of the *Adhishtanam*, and on the sidewalls of the passageway of the *gopurams* as at Chidambaram, Kumbakonam, Tiruvannamalai, Kanchipuram, Tiruvidaimarudur, and Jambukeswaram, dance *karanas* with accompanists on the flanks of the dancer abound. In places like Muzhaiyur, Darasuram and in temples with multi-storied *gopurams*, these dance figures become a common feature from the twelfth century onwards, right through the Chola, Pandya, Nayak and Vijayanagara periods.

8 Anukkiyar Paravai Nangiar and her gifts to the temple – A. R. E. 680 of 1919. See *South Indian Epigraphy*, Vol. XVII, nos. 764 and 762 (A.R.E. 707 and 705)

9 Rajaraja Natakam – *Santi Kootu*: S. R. Balasubrahmanyam, in his book, *Later Chola Temples*, gives on page 273 details of the inscriptions about *Santi kuttu* in the reign of Rajadhiraja II; it mentions that land was made available to meet the expenses, inter alia, to two women for performance of *Santi Kuttu* during the Tiruvadirai Festival in Vaikasi in front of the shrine of Sadira Vitanka Nayakar. He also refers to a gift of land to 'Ezhunattu Nangai' (young women of Ezhu Nadu) for nine performances of *Santi Kuttu* in the Chittirai Festival in homage to Lord Tiruvengaivayil Andar (A.R.E. 253 of 1914).

10 The entire inscription of Rajaraja I is from the Brihadeeshwara temple at Tanjavur. It contains even details of all the names of dancers and the various temples in different cities from which these *devadasis* were brought to serve in the Brihadeeshwara temple – S.I.I., II, no 6.

11 *Adavu-s*: This term still continues to be used for specified units of movement.

12 This expression is found as early as in the eleventh-twelfth centuries. In ancient days, the kings endowed the *Nattuvanar* with land called *nattuva-k-kani* as remuneration.

13 Sarfoji II and Shahaji were great composers and their compositions were first brought out in the Tanjore Saraswati Mahal Library publication. Guru Parvati Kumar was particularly interested in these Marathi compositions and did a lot to bring them to notice. For the first time, these were presented in the Bharatanatyam recital by Sucheta Chapekar, with the late Guru Kittappa Pillai providing the musical base for the compositions. This entire cluster of compositions, of *padas* and *darus*, was presented under the title, *Tyaga Prabandha*. Later with help from several Hindustani musicians, Sucheta presented the compositions of these kings in Hindustani *ragas* under the title, *Nrityaganga*. An experiment of doing Bharatanatyam to Hindustani music, the effort has evoked much praise for the manner in which Sucheta has retained the grammar of the dance form while setting it in the music of a different genre. Yet another Bharatanatyam dancer to do this successfully is Parul Jhaveri, a student of Parvati Kumar.

14 She herself hailed from a *devadasi* family and her passion to stamp out an institution, which had become the object of so much criticism, was one of the main driving forces in abolishing the system.

15 For more details on this subject, see *SRUTI*, Issue No. 5.

16 For more information on Rukmini Devi, see *SRUTI* issues 8,9 and 10 and Periya Sarada's book, *Kalakshetra –Rukmini Devi.*

17 Pandanallur was the headquarters of one of the administrative divisions of the Nayak Kingdom of Tanjavur apart from other important centres like Tiruvidaimarudur, Arantangi, and Tiruvarur etc., which became important centres of dance. Tanjavur was the starting point and the other schools, which were all a tributary of the one big river, developed into independent schools because of the individual greatness of Gurus. Meenakshi Sundaram Pillai at Pandanallur became the byword for the Pandanallur School, known for its strict adherence to form and profile of dance, with a linear geometry of great exactitude. Vazhuvoor was made popular by Vazhuvoor Ramiah Pillai whose approach to Bharatanatyam had more of grace, light-footed jumps and a fluidity which made the dance more lyrical. Kamala's dance epitomised his idea of Bharatanatyam. Now S. Kanaka in Delhi is a well-known exponent of this school. Late Rajaratnam Pillai and K. J. Sarasa are the two gurus of this school who have trained a large group of students. Vazhuvoor Ramiah Pillai became the first guru to be connected with the film dances and in the film, *Nam Iruvar*, his choreography for patriotic songs like *Vettri ettu dikkum etta* and *Aaduvome pallu paaduvome* became a hit.

Other gurus brought, in the course of their teaching careers, their own individualistic stylistic features to the dance. Today, while dancers learn from more than one guru, stylistic specificity is not easily traceable. Senior dancers who may have learnt under one school have also deviated from the guru's exact style by infusing their own features to the dance.

KATHAK

1 Read Kapila Vatsyayan's *Indian Classical Dances* on Kathak chapter.

2 Surdas, Nandadas, Kumbhandas, Paramanandadas, Chaturbhujdas, Krishnadas, Govindaswami and Chhitswami.

3 Reference is made in Sunil Kothari's book on Kathak.

4 Ashok Vajpeyi the ex bureaucrat whose association with Raigarh school of Kathak was very close, talked about this incident.

5 Ashok Vajpeyi was the person concerned.

6 I learnt all this in the course of interactions with Prerna Shrimali.

7 The book is *Aesthetics of Kathak*.

8 The word, *Nagmah*, has Arabic roots meaning sound, tone and melody. *Sruti 104* has a detailed article by late Nala Najan on the subject.

9 The dancer in question is Prerna.

10 Romani, the language of the gypsies (whose dance is Flamenco), is Indo-Aryan and retains Sanskrit and Hindi words. Philologists have placed the original home of the Romanis in the Gangetic plain, a diaspora around third century B.C. from northwestern India. They are equated with the Doms, said to be derived from *Doma* or *Domba*. Rom/Dom is a caste, a community with its own laws. These world wanderers appeared in Spain in 1425 and in Barcelona in 1447. During the war of the Crusades, they infiltrated gradually into different parts of Europe. Flamenco is said to come from the Flemish word or from the Arab *felchmengu*, that is, village singer or *fellah-ah-mengu*,meaning peasant in flight. Abhinavagupta refers to the 'Dombika' dance. Sanskrit texts of the eleventh, twelfth, and thirteenth centuries mention Domvaki and *Sangeet Makaranda* talks of *raga Domsuli* – a *Gauda raga* of the twelfth century.

ODISSI

1 'Antiquity of words: Odisa and Odiya' by P. Acharya (the Orissa Historical Reseach Journal Vol II, September 1953 and January 1954, nos. 3 and 4, pages 56-58).

2 *Tribhanga* – the main stance in Odissi where the head, torso and lower half of the body are deflected in opposed sideways positions to create the three-bend posture.

3 *Alasyakanya* refers to the indolent maiden and is represented in sculpture as woman in variously relaxed attitudes.

4 Dance is inspired by many of the attitudes in sculpture, depicting woman like *Alasya* (the indolent maiden), *Torana* (leaning on the doorway), *Mugdha* (innocent and inexperienced in love), *Manini* (resentful and offended), *Daalamaalika* (garlanding herself), *Padma-gandha* (smelling the lotus), *Darpana* (looking into the mirror), *Vinyaasa* or *Dhyaana karsita* (in meditation), *Ketaki-bharana* (with the *Ketaki* flower in the hair), *Matrumurti* (image of the mother), *Chamara* (holding a flywhisk), *Gunthana* (hiding behind the veil), *Nupur padika* (with ankle bells), and *Mardala* (playing the drum).

5 The foundation inscriptions for the three temples found their way, during British rule, to Kolkata Museum and from there to London. After the Orissa state was formed, efforts were made to retrieve the plaques. The Anantavasudeva foundation inscription is still in London, the slab relating to the Megheswar temple got fixed in the Anantavasudeva complex and the foundation plaque of the Brahmeswar temple is lost forever:

Sloka 16 of the foundation inscription of the temple of Anantavasudeva, Bhubaneswar, (1278 a.d.) reads :

Geetajnaa laya-taala narttana kala kaushalya leelaalaya /
Baalyaatyachyuta bhakti- bhaavitamatir-dattaanuroopashriyo //
Pitraa Haihayavamsajaaya shuchaye chandraapahaa chandrika /
putreeyam Paramarddi-naama bhajate kshatraaya ratnaanvitaa //

'Learned in songs, a seat of sport in skillful practice of arts of musical measure, beating of time, and the dance, and having a soul inspired with devotion to Achyuta (Vishnu), from childhood on wards, and the radiance and beauty of the moon, this daughter, Chandrika together with jewels was given (in marriage) by her father to PARAMARDDI, the knight (*Kshatriya*) and the scion of the Haihaya lineage (O H R J, Vol. V No.1, pp 68-69).

6 *Telinga Sampradaya* – literally, tradition of the Telugu region .

7 Oriya inscription reads: *Veerashri Gajapati Gowdeshwara Navakoti Karnata Kalavargesvara Prataparudra*

8 The bedtime service pertained to singing and dancing the *Geeta Govind* only, and was hence based on *abhinaya*.

9 Categorisation by Jivan Pani

10 What had come down from the *Mahari* and *Gotipua* lines was very limited and new hand symbols had to be devised for new ideas to be expressed. Only Mayadhar

Raut among the gurus had the benefit of systematised instruction in dance theory from Kalakshetra and his contribution was significant in this aspect

11 It is in this area that individual gurus have their subtle differences in perspective. Kelucharan Mohapatra forbids any movement of the hip and says that the sideway deflection below the waist has to be produced by the torso being moved sideways in the opposite direction. However, Debaprasad permits the slight hip bend. For Pankajcharan Das who generally supports the Kelucharan perspective, a slight hip deflection is also permissible in certain situations, particularly in his famous *Pancha Kanya* work based on the five women from Hindu mythology – Kunti, Tara, Mandodari, Ahalya and Draupadi

12 Pandit Raghunath Rath's *Natya Manorama* and *Sangitarnabha Chandrika*, Kavi Sri Haladhara Misra's *Sangeeta Kalpalatika*, Kavi Ratna Purushottama Misra's *Sangeeta Narayana*, Raja Harishchandra's *Sangeeta Muktabali* are the other texts, though later treatises more or less repeated the *Sangeet Ratnakara*.

KATHAKALI

1 *Katha* means story and *Kali* means play.
2 Kathakali *attakathas* or plays meant for the art form blend both Sanskrit and Malayalam in the libretto and the blend is called *Manipravalam*.
3 Vallathol was the literary editor for this newspaper in Malayalam.
4 This is an institution in many parts of Kerala where succession is traced through the female. While this had property implications, the woman was still in a very protected society where she was not allowed to engage in dancing as a profession. The exception was in the case of the *Kutiyattam Nangyar*.
5 The famous line reads: '*Kuvalaya Vilochane, Baale, Bhaimi, Kisalayodhare, Charusheele*' (O Lotus eyed young maiden, daughter of Bhima, with tender lips and winsome disposition). Great performers can embellish this one line and dance for any length of time.
6 There is a story within the main story that is rendered here, of an elephant being attacked simultaneously by a lion and a python. Fighting valiantly, the animal succumbs in the end. This episode is dramatised in the play by the actor as Bhima. Kalamandalam Ramankutty Nair is an expert in this sequence.
7 See also Chapter on Mohini Attam, where there is a paragraph on *Sopanam*.
8 The Guru heads the faculty at International Centre for Kathakali and is one of the most respected performer-gurus of Kathakali. He has trained under renowned gurus Keezhpatam Kumaran Nair, Kondiveeti Narayanan Nair and Thekinkatil Ramunni Nair.
9 Maya Rao has been the student of Guru Sadanam Balakrishnan for years. She is primarily a theatre expert and is working with the National School.

MOHINI ATTAM

1 A festival is celebrated beginning on the day of the Tiruvonam star in the month of Dhanus till the birth of the Tiruvatira star, and Thiruvathirakali is performed on all these days.
2 G. Venu in his book on Mohini Attam mentions that the Kerala *devadasi*, when thirteen years old, was given 'in a token marriage to God', according to the *penkettu* custom. Obviously, there is a difference of opinion on the *devadasi* being married to the temple deity.
3 '*Chitram ranghe vinihitapada*
    Chittarangeshu yoonam
    Nrithyanthyavir lalithamabala
    Yatra sandhyolsa veshu'
    (At dusk, the girls danced at the Trikkanamatilakam temple with abandon, the dance appealing to the eyes and leaving an imprint on the mind. The graceful dance made for a colourful picture in the courtyard.)
4 Leela Omcheri, noted *Sopanam* specialist, and scholar advances this view.
5 Record 107, Central Archives, Thiruvananthapuram, is about an order issued in the early nineteenth century during the regency of Princess Gouri Parvati Bai of a Mohini Attam teacher Ayyappa Panikkar engaged to teach four girls in the *Natakasala*.
6 A typical example is Iraiyaman Tampi's '*Entaho Vallabha inneram mauna bhavam – entaparadham ceytu jnan*' in *Asaveri ragam* set to *Adi talam*. ('Why, my husband, this silence for so long, what offence have I committed?')
    Another example is Swait Tirunal's lyric '*Kantanodu chennu melle*' in *Nilambari ragam* and *Rupaka talam* ('Oh my *sakhi*, go, convince my husband with sweet words about my plight.')
7 There is another version of the myth which says that the *Asuras*' downfall came with Mohini insisting that Bhasmasura swear his love for her by placing his hand on his head.
8 Kavalam Narayana Panikkar is firmly of this view
9 See Kanak Rele's *Mohini Attam: The Lyrical Dance* – page 114, for the full Malayalam quotation.
10 The dancer also did an item called *Polikai*, which was just a way of collecting money

from the audience by spreading a cloth. In Kerala's glove puppet tradition, in which the puppets are designed like the Mohini Attam dancers, this way of spreading a cloth for money collection is accepted even today.

11 See reference to this in chapter on Bharatanatyam.
12 *Sopanam* specialist Leela Omcheri's view.
13 See book by mother and daughter *Keralattile Laasyarachanakal*

MANIPURI

1 The word *Lai-hoi-lauba* splits up thus: *Lai* is God, *Hoi* is Sound and *Lauba* is shouting or singing
2 These gods are regarded as Manipuri counterparts of Siva and Parvati. Similar to the myth of the Hindu God, Ganesa.
2a In one of the Chapka villages in a regional version of the *Lai-haraoba* celebrations, the biggest *Pung* instrument is kept and worshipped. The dance is supposed to have been created from the time of the migration, which came from the east – the *Nongpok Haram*. It is regarded as special, though nobody is allowed to see the dance.
3 My interactions with Manipuri guru Singhajit Singh have yielded special insights into Manipuri.
4 There is also a theory put forward by some scholars that Vaishnavism came to Manipur from Burma (Myanmar) and there is a legend about King Pong of Burma who rubbed his body with a stone and contacted an incurable skin disease. The stone was identified as *Vishnu-chakra*. The skin condition could be cured only after it was propitiated by a Brahmin. After a long search a Brahmin performing his evening prayers (*sandhya vandanam*) in front of the river, was identified and his worship of the *Vishnu-chakra* cured the king who became a convert. His faith spread to Manipur, much before the reformers came from India.
4a Here, it is Krishna as Jagannath, with Balabhadra and Subhadra, exactly as in the Orissan Rath Jatra, but with each temple here having its own procession.
4b Krishna is woken up from a long sleep during the monsoon.
5 It is believed that the statue of Radha has the likeness of Bimbawati, the daughter of King Bhagyachandra who was the first dancer as Radha in *Manipuri Raasa*.
6 For further information on the meaning behind the geometry of the square and the circle refer to Kapila Vatsyayan's *Square and the Circle of the Indian Arts*.
7 Spinning on knees (*jaanu bhrahmaris*) or spinning the body in the air (*Akash bhramaris*) are special to Manipuri.
8 Showing how images from Nature are so much a part of the dance.
9 That this can be rendered only during night has made it rare today.
10 Like a coiled spring, the dancer's body raises or lowers itself in keeping with the motif of the intertwined snake.
11 Yaithing Konu, Leiman and Ingel-Lei, Babrubahan, Yayati, Kumar Sambhav, Shakuntala, Arjun Parajay, Savitri are some. In *Chhaya Purush*, he experimented with light-shade effects.
12 Creation like *Tasher Desh* based on *Rabindra Sangeet* was very popular with certain audiences.
13 Rajkumar Singhajit Singh agrees that in all his years of teaching, he has encountered very few non-Manipur people who have come forward to learn the dance.

KUCHIPUDI

1 The families mentioned are Bhagavatulu, Bokka, Darbha, Eleswarupu, Hari, Josyula, Mahankali, Pasumarti, Peddibhatla, Polepeddi, Vallabha Josyula, Vedantam, Vempati, Vemu and Vonukurti. Descendants of Mahankali, Vempati, Vedantam, Pasumarti, and Eleswarapu continue in the tradition.
2 *Agraharams* (Brahmin settlements) like Adityakuchi, Doddanakuchi, Chippanakuchi find mention in the twelfth-century *Basavapuranam* by Palkuriki Somanatha.
3 Arudra's views, published first in 1986 in the Institute of Traditional Cultures of Madras and later updated in *SRUTI 54* on 'Background and Evolution of Kuchipudi'.
4 *Madalu Pattu*, a sequence of love potions and charms in an old manuscript copy of *Bhama Kalapam*, in possession of Vedantam Chalamiah, the great grandfather of the Kuchipudi doyen, Vedantam Prahlada Sarma, in which a lyric (*daru*) in *Suddha Saveri raga* has the name Siddhendra in the signature line. Arudra came across this manuscript by chance ('Lingering questions and some fashionable fallacies' – *SRUTI 115*).
5 '*Sharanamachyutapura Nivasa Swami Varada Raja Prabhu*' – so goes the lyric.
6 *Manduka Sabdam* by Kasinathaiyya and *Prahlada Pattabhisheka Sabdam* by Venkatarama Sastry are still rendered quite often in Kuchipudi recitals.
7 The pleated braid (*jada*) is supposed to have been worn by Vishnu when he assumed the female form of Mohini and came down to earth. When he reverted to his divine self as Vishnu, in his incarnation as Krishna, he gave it to Satyabhama. There are other similar versions about the relevance of the braid.
8 Mohan Khokar writes about the incident in his 'Kuchipudi Then and Now' in *SRUTI 153*.

Puranamityeya na sadhu sarvam
Na chapi kavyam navamityabaddham
Santah Parikshanyataradbhajante
Mudhah Parapratyaneya Buddhih

Malavikagnimitra of Kalidasa, Act I, Verse 2

144 ————————●————————

Nothing should be taken as good
or acceptable merely because it is old

Nothing should be treated as bad merely
because it is new

Great men accept the one or the other
after careful examination or deliberation

It is only a fool who has his mind
led by the beliefs of others.

(translation by A. K. Krishna Rao)

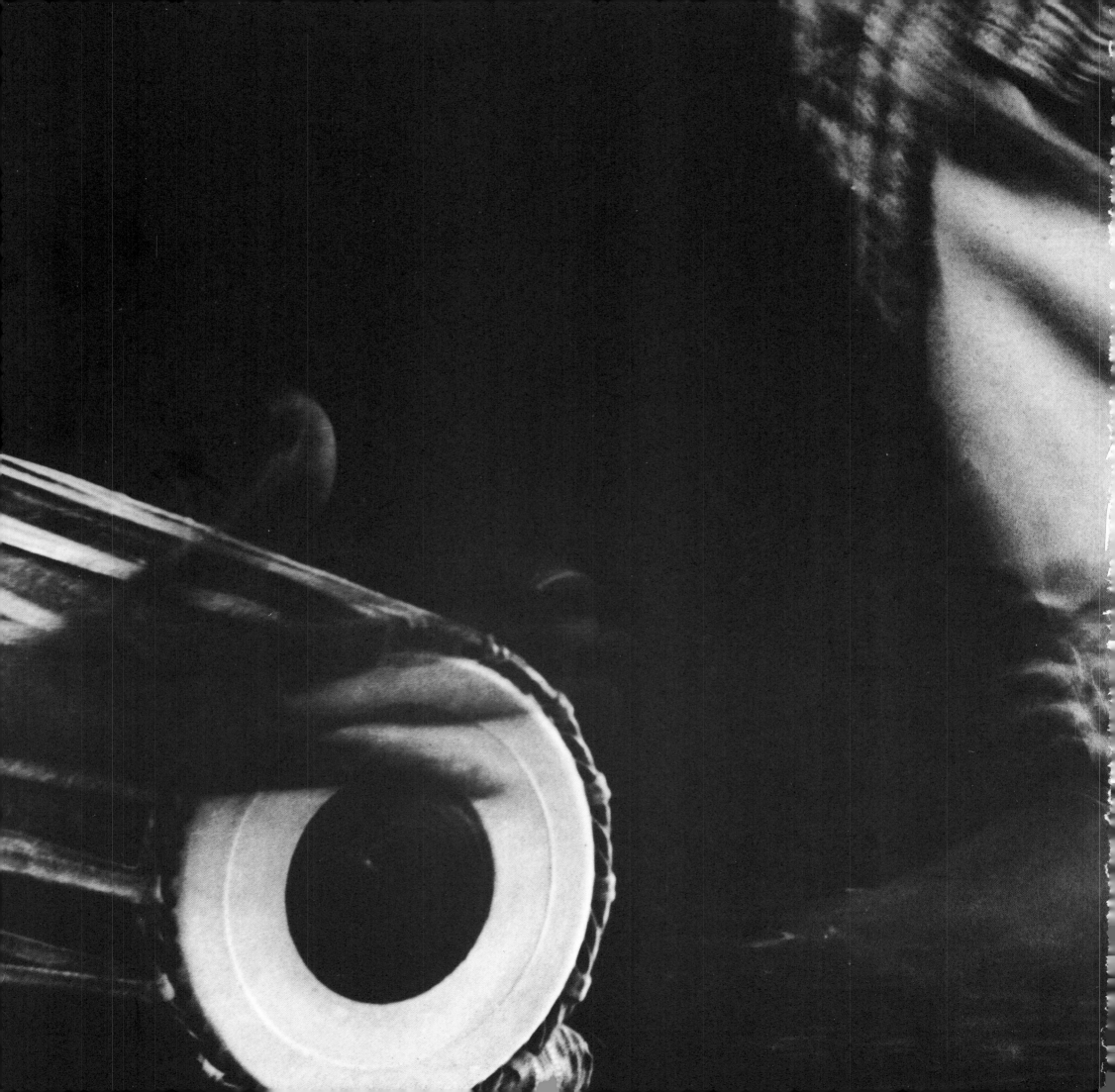